FOREVER
WOLVES

FOREVER WOLVES

A celebration of Wolverhampton Wanderers' 125th anniversary

by
David Instone

Express & Star
and
Shropshire Star

Thomas Publications

T
P

First published in Great Britain in September, 2002, by
Thomas Publications, PO Box 17, Newport,
Shropshire, England, TF10 7WT

ISBN 0 9512051 4 5

Printed and bound by Butler & Tanner, Frome, Somerset

Contents

Foreword

By Bert Williams, Wolves and England

EACH time the Express & Star bring out one of their quality publications on Wolverhampton Wanderers, I assume that's finally it: the well of old photographs on the club has run dry. Then, two years later, out comes another book, containing many more pictures we haven't previously seen!

Having had a sneak preview in the spring of 2002, I'm glad to say that the content of this latest tribute to the club - produced by sports reporter David Instone in conjunction with the Express & Star and Shropshire Star - is packed with material that I have never had the pleasure of seeing anywhere before.

It is a treasure chest of memories for Wolves lovers everywhere, including the many former players like myself who will be delighted to take a walk down Memory Lane and deliberate over more than 300 poignant images of the past.

Photographs of games and incidents I had long forgotten are here in abundance and I know my contemporaries from the 1940s and 1950s will have many happy hours flicking through the pages. No doubt the questions will be reeled off when the club's Former Players Association next meet up: Is it really 50 years ago that that match was played? Was so-and-so still playing then? And, most commonly, did we really look like that?

I'm sure Wolves players from other decades and other generations will find just the same satisfaction as we will and be glad that they have something new in print to show their friends and families from their Molineux days. It is a fitting record for us all of very, very happy days.

The publication is well timed, coming out as it does in Wolverhampton Wanderers' 125th year. It is a most appropriate souvenir of this happy anniversary.

We wish the Express & Star, Shropshire Star and author good luck with the latest venture and, as ever, pass on all our best to Sir Jack Hayward and everyone else at the club, for the present season and the future.

And, of course, we wonder whether there will be one more nostalgia book like this to look forward to at some later date.......

Introduction

FEW English football clubs can boast the richness of history that is the proud possession of Wolverhampton Wanderers.

Mention that 22-letter name in Great Britain, Europe and beyond, and eyes will light up in recognition of the pre-war eminence under Major Frank Buckley, the fantastic deeds of the Stan Cullis-inspired 1950s, the great cup-fighting days of the 1970s and early 1980s, or the general prominence this founder member of the Football League has occupied in many other decades before and since.

It is now 125 years since this institution of the sporting world arrived on the scene and we at the Express & Star and Shropshire Star are delighted to mark this important anniversary in 2002 with a book we believe does justice to the memory of men like Broadbent, Bull, Cullis, Flowers, Gardiner, Hancocks, Mullen, Richards, Slater, Swinbourne, Williams and Wright.

There have been plenty of worthy publications on Wolves but none can have offered supporters a look at so many 'new' old pictures, for this is very much a delve into the hidden archives. We have crammed well over 300 photographs into the 192 pages of this nostalgic trawl through the club's history and could not have done any more to ensure the highest possible exclusivity of the content.

If any picture within these covers has appeared in a previous Wolves book, rest assured it has slipped through the net. Any photograph we know to have appeared in a previous Molineux-related publication has been cast aside and replaced by one that hasn't.

The vast majority have come out of the Express & Star library or that of our sister paper, the Ketley-based Shropshire Star, whose help is gratefully acknowledged and which remains a valuable day-to-day source of information for Wolves fans on that side of the Midlands.

Other pictures have been generously loaned to us by ex-players Cyril Sidlow, Bert Williams and, in particular, Eddie Stuart. They receive our thanks for their kindness in helping us bring this project to fruition, as does former World Cup final referee Jack Taylor. The personal collection of the late Joe Gardiner also has a good airing within these chapters. It being a Wolves book, Molineux historian Graham Hughes, Former Players Association secretary Peter Creed and statistician Tony Matthews have also each played a big part. Eddie Holding's identification skills were much appreciated as well.

Our friends in other newspaper offices in cities ranging from Newcastle to Southampton, and Norwich to Cardiff, have opened their doors to us and made sure that many photographs that West Midlands-based fans will never previously have seen even in old newspapers could take their place within these pages.

London-based photographer Ken Coton has also been well to the fore with action shots of various Wolves games against Fulham and, from further north, we are happy to record similar appreciation to memorabilia collector Denis Clareborough. On a personal note, the author would like to thank Express & Star librarian Fran Cartwright for her support, his wife Liz and his work colleague David Cooper for their technical expertise, Sports Editor Steve Gordos for his encouragement and proof reading and another long-time Molineux regular, John Lalley, who has given up several weekend days and many post-school hours in going through these pictures and helping with identification and detail.

The scanning, as usual, has been the domain of the Express & Star's Paul Wilson while John Hackney and his colleagues in the paper's artist department have designed the front and back covers.

Last but by no means least, it should be pointed out that the famous and in some cases forgotten incidents portrayed in this book have been captured, in the main, by a host of fine Express & Star and Shropshire Star photographers past and present.

Memories of Molineux, Talking With Wolves, The Bully Years, The A to Z of Wolves, Sir Jack.......the Express & Star have joined forces with Breedon Books and Thomas Publications to produce a variety of books chronicling the club's proud history. Now we believe we have another winner with Forever Wolves.

Enjoy the journey through the first 125 years of Wolverhampton Wanderers......

Early Days

A Wolves team picture from the early 1900s - a period when the side were run by long-serving secretary-manager Jack Addenbrooke. At the time, the club were also-rans in the First Division and made no great strides in the FA Cup either. They were relegated at the end of the 1905-06 campaign and were to spend no fewer than 22 seasons, including one in Division Three North, outside English football's top flight.

PLAY UP WOLVES

WOLVERHAMPTON WANDERERS.
English Cup Team, 1908.

LUNN (GOAL)
JONES   COLLINS (BACKS)
HUNT WOOLDRIDGE BISHOP (HALF BACKS)
HARRISON SHELTON HEDLEY RADFORD PEDLEY
(FORWARDS)

Wembley wasn't on the football map when Wolves won the FA Cup in 1908 - but they still had to show the London audience what they were capable of on the road to glory. After overcoming Bradford City, Bury, Swindon and Stoke in the opening four rounds, they beat Southampton 2-0 in the semi-final at Chelsea and then defeated Newcastle at Crystal Palace. The final was won 3-1 in front of 74,967, thanks to goals by Reverend Kenneth Hunt, Billy Harrison and George Hedley.

The tunnel area is unmistakably Molineux, even if some of the advertising boards, the other bits of décor and even the clothes fashions are less familiar. This atmospheric scene was captured in the 1920s - a time when Wolves were marooned in the Second Division after winning Division Three North under the management of George Jobey in 1923-24. They didn't win promotion back to the top flight until 1931-32.

Hi, I'm Alex Scott! There's a fitting handshake from the 6ft 4in goalkeeper as he is introduced to his new team-mates at Molineux following his £1,250 signing from Burnley in 1936. The Liverpudlian played 129 games in a stay that also contained several dozen outings in wartime. Scott, who was later in service as a police detective, appeared for Wolves in the 1939 FA Cup final and in sides who finished League runners-up in 1937-38 and 1938-39.

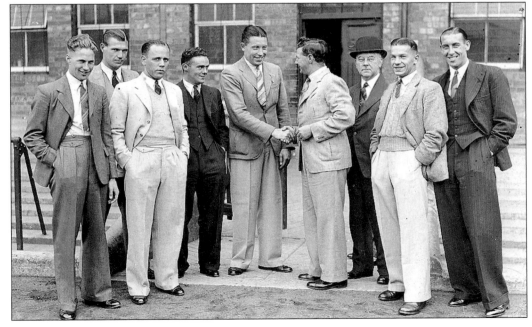

Pre-War Boom

Two images of Wolves' First Division home game against Derby on September 6, 1937. Above: Former policeman Gordon Clayton lets the Rams keeper know he's around with the sort of robust challenge that was legal at the time. Below: A desperate overhead kick keeps Wolves out near the end of a game which ended 2-2 five days after they had won 2-1 at the Baseball Ground. Clayton scored in both matches and had the tremendous record of 39 goals in 55 first-team appearances for the club between 1933 and 1938. He was then sold to Aston Villa and helped them to promotion from the Second Division before the outbreak of war. The 1937-38 campaign was Wolves' best up to that time, Major Frank Buckley's emerging side finishing second in the top flight, only a point behind Arsenal. They would have won the title had it not been for a last-day 1-0 defeat at Sunderland. Pictures courtesy of Derby Evening Telegraph.

Even before their 1938-39 run to the FA Cup final, Wolves were in the habit of giving their players days out like this in grander surroundings to break the routine of training. Lining up for this team photograph with a difference are (from left) Alex Scott, Bryn Jones, Stan Cullis, George Ashall, Tom Smalley, Jack Kirkham, Dennis Westcott, Tom Galley, Jack Taylor, Teddy Maguire, Frank Taylor (Jack's brother), Joe Gardiner, Bill Morris and Harold Thompson.

It's colours v whites late 1930s style. Back row from left: Unknown, Joe Gardiner, Bill Parker, Jack Kirkham, Harry Brown, Frank Taylor, Jim Myers, Bert Barlow, Unknown. Middle: Unknown, Bill Morris, Wilson, Cyril Sidlow, Alex Scott, Anderson, Bradbourn, Tom Galley, Unknown. Front: Teddy Maguire, Dicky Dorsett, Stan Cullis, Horace Wright, Harold Thompson, Alex McIntosh, Dennis Westcott, Billy Wrigglesworth. In the three seasons immediately prior to the war, Wolves finished fifth, second and second in Division One. Keeper Sidlow played seven times for Wales, including a famous ocasion at The Hawthorns against England when Bert Williams was in goal for the home side.

Wolves face the camera in Prague before playing a friendly against Sparta during their hectic, five-match tour of Europe in 1938. The hostilities were an ever-increasing threat at the time of the 15-day trip, that took Major Frank Buckley's players by train to Belgium, Germany, Hungary, Poland, Austria and France, as well as the Czechoslovakian capital. And the prospect of war clearly didn't prevent a big turn-out at this game, which was followed by others in Budapest, Katowice, Vienna and Paris. Pictured are (back row from left) Bill Morris, Dennis Westcott, George Ashall, Alex Scott, Jack Taylor, Tom Galley. Front: Dicky Dorsett, Bill Parker, Bryn Jones, Joe Gardiner, Teddy Maguire.

An unusual Molineux view in the 1930s as the famous old stadium is seen without its massive South Bank structure. That was built shortly after this picture was taken at a training match on a smoggy Wolverhampton morning. The rest of the ground's covered areas are very much in keeping with what became familiar for four and a half decades, though, with the North Bank, Molineux Street and Waterloo Road sides already well established.

Double Runners-up

A policeman on horseback urges spectators off the pitch during Wolves' FA Cup semi-final clash with Grimsby on March 25, 1939. The game was played at Old Trafford, where the gate of 76,962 still stands as a record, and was subjected to a delay before play could resume. Major Frank Buckley's Wolves had beaten Bradford, Leicester, Liverpool and Everton to reach the last four. Pictures courtesy of Grimsby Evening Telegraph.

Tom Galley turns in triumph after driving home the semi-final penalty that underlined Wolves' supremacy and helped set up a crushing 5-0 victory over a Grimsby side who were also in the top flight at the time. The other four goals came from the brilliant Dennis Westcott, who netted no fewer than 124 times for the club in 144 appearances. Wolves had also hammered the Mariners twice in the League over Christmas, 4-2 away on Boxing Day and 5-0 at Molineux the following day.

Four more photos from the Wolves v Grimsby semi-final. Top: Dicky Dorsett steams goalwards, only to collide (middle) with keeper George Moulson and go down in a heap in an incident that left the forward being attended to (above) by Alex McIntosh. The fact that the Humbersiders had to use one of their outfield players as a replacement keeper - in the days before substitutes were permitted - merely confirmed Wolves' dominance of the tie. In the winners' line-up was left-winger Jimmy Mullen, who played in the quarter-final and semi-final despite being only a few weeks past his 16th birthday. Pictures courtesy of Grimsby Evening Telegraph.

It's not hi-tech training - but it obviously worked! Wolves' players are about to leave their starting blocks in a sprinting session on the Molineux pitch during the late 1930s. From left are: Stan 'Dizzy' Burton, Teddy Maguire, Alex McIntosh, Dicky Dorsett, Frank Taylor, Stan Cullis, Dennis Westcott, Frank Morris, Joe Gardiner, Alex Scott, Tom Galley. The trainer is Jack Davies. Wolves were about to hit the heights in English football under the management of Major Frank Buckley.

DOUBLE RUNNERS-UP

An FA Cup final shocker for Wolves as they are humbled 4-1 by Portsmouth in 1939. Pompey had trailed in 17th in the First Division while Major Frank Buckley's team were runners-up to Everton. But that counted for little and Alex Scott's full-length dive was not enough to stop Bert Barlow opening the scoring with a cracker. Barlow had been sold from Molineux to Fratton Park only ten weeks earlier! The war and the fact the competition did not resume until 1946-47 meant Pompey held the Cup longer than any other club in history.

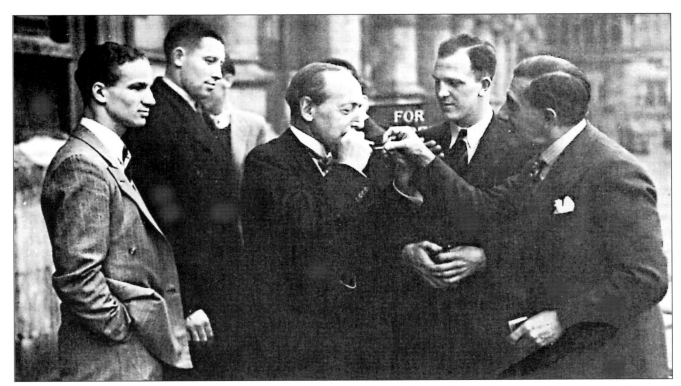

Stan Cullis (second right) stands between MPs Sir Robert Bird and Geoffrey Mander as Wolves' players are shown round the Houses of Parliament following their 4-1 FA Cup final defeat against Portsmouth on April 29, 1939. On the far left is Frank Taylor, with keeper Alex Scott next to him. Pompey claimed an autograph book passed among their players before the game after previously being sent round the other dressing-room had 'shaky' Wolves signatures in it - supposed proof of their opponents' nerves!

Molineux is the sunny setting for an unusual and friendly meeting of cultures as Wolves' players take a breather during training to extend a warm welcome to some visitors from overseas. The size of the balls that form the subject of the conversation are clearly different to what the squad were used to but the smiles from both sides of the divide are unmistakable.

Wolves keeper Cyril Sidlow punches clear to halt an Albion attack on a wintry afternoon at Molineux during the long years of wartime football. Sidlow, who was also a fine cricketer, went on to win League Championship honours and play in an FA Cup final for Liverpool after leaving behind a Wolves camp who won the Wartime League Cup at the expense of Sunderland in 1941-42 after beating the Baggies 7-0 in a two-legged semi-final.

Post-War Emergence

Molineux is well populated again shortly after the war as the sliding Dennis Westcott and Jimmy Mullen (left) bear down on Sunderland's goal. Westcott lost some of his finest Football League years to the hostilities while Mullen's long first-team career was launched in 1938-39 and ended an incredible 20 seasons and 486 senior games later. The Newcastle-born left-winger also played 12 times for England from 1947 to 1954.

Danger in the mud for Wolves as Bert Williams leaves his line and challenges Arsenal's Ronnie Rooke in the 1-1 draw at Highbury on December 28, 1946. Billy Wright, Tom Galley and Stan Cullis are also on hand. The club, under the management of Ted Vizard, had kicked off League football after the war by thrashing Arsenal 6-1 at Molineux on the opening day of 1946-47, all six goals coming in the second half on a day Williams played his first League game for Wolves.

Gentleman Joe

IN SO many ways, Joe Gardiner is the forgotten man when the plaudits are handed out in recognition of Wolverhampton Wanderers' glory years. But not among the many players whose careers he touched.

Those whose working lives he helped to shape have always been full of admiration for his essential role in building and maintaining the truly great Molineux sides of the 1930s, 1940s and 1950s.

Like Stan Cullis - his half-back colleague in the pre-war and wartime years - playing honours in terms of League Championship medals and FA Cup triumphs eluded him. Glory duly came, though, as with the great manager himself, after vacating the spotlight and crossing the divide into the backroom.

County Durham-bred Gardiner was born in one World War and had a big chunk taken out of his playing career by the other one. But what fantastic service he still gave the club on the pitch and off it!

He moved to the West Midlands as an amateur in 1932, signed professional the year after at 17 and made his Football League debut at Albion in February, 1935, completing his full graduation from the ranks of Buckley's Babes by the time he faced Portsmouth in Wolves' shock FA Cup final defeat of 1939.

The previous year, he had represented the English Football League against the Scottish League at Molineux and might well have followed Cullis into the full national team had Hitler not wiped out six years of what would have been the prime of his playing life.

He remained part of Wolves' side during the war but those few dozen outings during the hostilities, on top of almost 140 League and FA Cup appearances for the club, were a relatively modest tally for a player who could easily have made two or three times the number.

Undaunted, he accompanied Cullis into coaching in the days when trainers were something other than fashion items! They were the men who assisted the manager and also ran on to the field with a bucket and 'magic' sponge to attend to injured players.

Wolves stars of various generations regarded Gardiner as the quiet, sensitive one behind the Iron Man boss. "Joe was a man you could talk to and who would calm things down," said former Molineux and England forward Dennis Wilshaw in an Express & Star interview after Gardiner's death in July, 1997. "And he was a Wolves man through and through.

"I think his influence on the team has been greatly underplayed. We were a long-ball team under Stan, and Joe always backed him in his views on how the game should be played. But he did much more. If he spotted any faults that needed ironing out in your play, he was always prepared to spend time helping.

"We had so much respect for him as a coach because people then were forever talking about the wonderful Tom Galley-Stan Cullis-Joe Gardiner half-back line at Wolves before the war."

Keeper Bert Williams echoed the thoughts of his former England international colleague. "I never knew anyone have a bad word about Joe," he said.

"Coaching wasn't what it is today. It was really just about keeping everyone fit. But he was the one who was always there. Stan was obviously away on occasions but we knew we had someone else we could trust and get help from."

Wolves players of the halcyon 1949-60 period recall Cullis's right-hand man as a figure of cool assurance who played a major part in the winning of three League titles and two FA Cups. Gardiner was a man the young players would look up to because he took the time out to assist them in their development. 'Thoughtful' is another word that springs easily to mind - and that doesn't just mean the players who took Wolves to the dizzy heights five decades ago.

Remarkably, he remained at the club for around half a century; an amazing story of loyalty! He became chief scout after his trainer days were at an end and no less a Molineux name than John Richards attributes much of the reason for his own arrival at Wolves in the late 1960s to the care and consideration Gardiner showed him when he had to choose between Derby, Sheffield Wednesday and the West Midlands.

"Joe was a fabulous man," the striker said. "He was my first point of contact with Wolves and, thanks to him, my first impression was that I would be happy here. He was very sincere and there could not have been a better man to sell the club to me."

Gardiner finally retired in 1981 and remained a close friend of the club until his passing 16 years later at the age of 81. Compared with the likes of Billy Wright, Bert Williams, Ron Flowers, Bill Slater and Cullis, he may not be considered a household name by subsequent generations. But he was Wolves through and through and a legend in his own right.

Many of the pictures in this particular section, plus various others elsewhere, are from Joe's personal collection, which was passed to the Express & Star and then happily handed on to Wolves' museum for the enjoyment of the masses. Hopefully, they act as a fitting summary of his unique 50 years with the club.

Training time at Molineux as (from left) Bill Morris, Tom Galley, Stan Cullis, Joe Gardiner and Frank Taylor practise their skills. Morris, a centre-half who became a right-back with Cullis's emergence, played 197 League and FA Cup games - a tally that would have been a lot higher had it not been for the outbreak of war. He also played three times for England. Taylor played in the 1939 Cup final but wasn't seen with the club after the hostilities, subsequently managing Stoke.

Joe Gardiner listens in as Stan Cullis chooses Molineux's famous players' tunnel area for a talk-in with he, physio George Palmer, trainer Jack Davies and reserve trainer Jack Dowen shortly after his appointment as Wolves manager. Cullis was upgraded to boss in the summer of 1948, having had a year as assistant to Ted Vizard following his retirement as a player with the heartbreaking defeat at home to Liverpool in May, 1947 - the match that settled the destination of the League Championship.

Watching another drive fly down the middle of the fairway! Joe (centre) and Sammy Smyth admire Billy Wright's golf skills as Wolves, having thrashed Aston Villa 4-0 on Christmas Day and lost 5-1 at Villa Park two days later, take a rest and recuperation break at Blackpool early in their triumphant FA Cup run of 1948-49. They had just thrashed Chesterfield 6-0 at Molineux in the third round.

It's not just football!

Johnny Hancocks, the popular Shropshire-born right-winger who played three times for England as well as 378 times for Wolves, decides to stay out of the aerial fray in this light-hearted summer-time Molineux training session supervised by Gardiner (left). No wonder! He measured only 5ft 4in - a frame clearly not suited to this 'basketball' stint. Hancocks' slight build also made his cannonball-like shooting all the more remarkable.

Joe Gardiner (left) and Bill Shorthouse (right) are up among the 'leaders' during this unusual shot from summer, 1949, when the FA Cup winners headed for Ireland on an end-of-season trip. Bilston-born Shorthouse, played 376 matches for the club and picked up a League Championship medal as well as Cup honours. Third from the left on the front row is former Express & Star reporter Phil Morgan, known in the newspaper for many years as Commentator.

Another photo souvenir from the trip to Ireland, with players and officials suitably attired against the unseasonal weather. Note the unusual mode of transport partly in view on the left and the particularly relaxed pose of Wembley goalscorer Jesse Pye (front row, far right). Joe Gardiner is fourth left on the back row, with Stan Cullis two places to the right.

An eager learner and an excellent coach and role model. Gentleman Joe Gardiner has the full attention in these two pictures of one of his many star 'pupils.' A young Ron Flowers, who was to go on to play 49 times for the England senior side and be part of their World Cup-winning squad in 1966, is seen here studying the coaching manual with his mentor and then putting into practice what he has learned.

Nervous times on the touchline during Wolves' ground-breaking tour of Russia during the summer of 1955. Fitness coach Frank Morris is pictured in the middle while Joe Gardiner settles for biting his nails rather than following physio George Palmer in lighting up!

FA Cup Glory

ONCE bitten, twice shy......Wolves weren't going to blow it for a second time when the chance of FA Cup glory re-presented itself in 1948-49.

The stigma of failure and embarrassment from their Wembley clash with Portsmouth exactly ten years earlier lived on with fans, with Stan Cullis - now manager rather than centre-half supreme - and with surviving members of staff.

But, come the late-April day they faced Leicester at football's spiritual home, there was to be no repeat upset. Following the humiliating 4-1 defeat against unfancied Pompey, Wolves ensured the return to the Twin Towers went very much to the form-book.

Leicester were a Second Division club at the time and Wolves one of the high-fliers in the First, and the outcome was a 3-1 victory for the hot favourites; some major silverware to show off at last round the streets of Wolverhampton for a club who had not won the League Championship at that point and who hadn't lifted the FA Cup for 41 long years.

We now know it was the start of a golden age for Wolves. Fans lucky enough to see the Cup journey unfold witnessed glimpses of the might that was to sweep aside all before the club over the next decade.

There was very much a northern feel to that glorious 1948-49 run. Chesterfield, Sheffield United and Liverpool had been overpowered in a tide of goals by the middle of February and, after Jimmy Mullen's third and last goal in that season's competition had edged out Albion at Molineux, Manchester United were shown the exit door in a quite epic semi-final spanning two games.

Wolves, the club who had almost become great before the war, were the scourge of England.

A posed photograph in front of the old Waterloo Road Stand before morning training at Molineux in 1949, the year Wolves finished sixth in the First Division as well as lifting the FA Cup. Pictured are (from left) Bill Crook, Roy Pritchard, Jesse Pye, Bill Shorthouse, Sammy Smyth, Billy Wright, Bert Williams, Johnny Hancocks, Laurie Kelly, Jimmy Dunn, Jimmy Mullen and trainer Joe Gardiner.

Rival skippers Jimmy Hagan and Billy Wright come face to face as they toss up before Wolves' FA Cup fourth-round tie away to Sheffield United on January 29, 1949. A gate of 49,796 had Bramall Lane bulging but the home fans went home disappointed after their side had lost 3-0 to goals by Johnny Hancocks (2) and Jimmy Dunn. Wolves had thrashed Chesterfield in round three and were to go much further in the competition......

An anxious Molineux moment as an effort by Liverpool's Jack Balmer grazes the bar during the FA Cup fifth-round tie on February 12, 1949. Looking on for Wolves are (from left) Jimmy Dunn, Billy Wright, Bill Shorthouse, Lol Kelly, Roy Pritchard and Bert Williams. Wolves won 3-1 to gain revenge for their title heartbreak against the Merseysiders in 1946-47, when they were sunk by striker Albert Stubbins - pictured here between Shorthouse and Kelly. Picture courtesy of Liverpool Post and Echo.

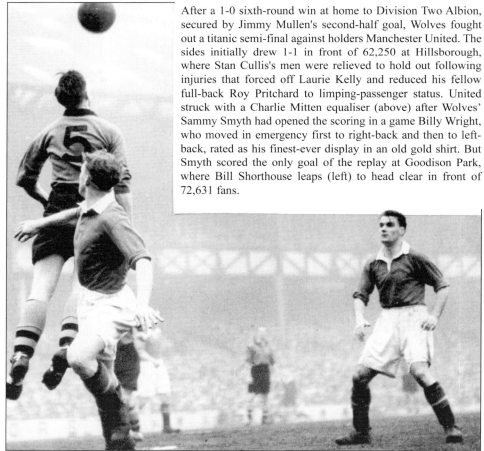

After a 1-0 sixth-round win at home to Division Two Albion, secured by Jimmy Mullen's second-half goal, Wolves fought out a titanic semi-final against holders Manchester United. The sides initially drew 1-1 in front of 62,250 at Hillsborough, where Stan Cullis's men were relieved to hold out following injuries that forced off Laurie Kelly and reduced his fellow full-back Roy Pritchard to limping-passenger status. United struck with a Charlie Mitten equaliser (above) after Wolves' Sammy Smyth had opened the scoring in a game Billy Wright, who moved in emergency first to right-back and then to left-back, rated as his finest-ever display in an old gold shirt. But Smyth scored the only goal of the replay at Goodison Park, where Bill Shorthouse leaps (left) to head clear in front of 72,631 fans.

Many Wolves and Leicester fans went early to London on FA Cup final day to take in some sights before the big match. This group, complete with rattle, are pictured at Horse Guards Parade.

Into the arena walk Wolves and Leicester, led by their managers and captains - Stan Cullis and Billy Wright for Wolves, Johnny Duncan and Norman Plummer for Leicester. In view behind Wright are Roy Pritchard and Bill Shorthouse. The attendance at a partially roof-less Wembley was 98,920.

Two views of the goal that started to put Wolves' name on the Cup for the third time. The 1893 and 1908 winners draw first blood as Jesse Pye, scorer of 95 goals in his 209 Wolves games, breaks the deadlock with a superb 12th minute header (above). The goal eased any nerves the favourites might have experienced and had Pye running away in delight (below) in search of provider Johnny Hancocks.

Wolves are pictured on the attack again but this effort flashes a couple of feet wide of the post as keeper Bradley covers.

Billy Wright, playing in his only FA Cup final and appearing against the club he represented in wartime football, watches this safe catch by Bert Williams that ends a Leicester attack.

The ball is in the Wolves net despite the efforts of the diving Bert Williams - but he needn't have worried. The linesman in the distance has his flag up and this 'goal' by Ken Chisholm was disallowed on a marginal offside decision. Bill Shorthouse is the player turning appealingly towards the referee. It was to prove Leicester's last real foothold in the game.

Belfast-born Sammy Smyth has his sights on goal in this aerial challenge that is thwarted by a decisive punch by Bradley.

The luck of the Irish! Smyth gets his sights just right as he crashes in the killer third goal to complete the scoring after Leicester had pulled one back. This left-foot shot came at the end of a magnificent run and is still hailed as one of the finest goals ever seen at Wembley. The forward won nine full international caps and scored 43 goals in 116 first-team games for Wolves from 1947 to 1951.

* The famous 1949 Sporting Star front page announcing that it's a day of joy and Wembley glory for Cullis's Wolves.

Mmmm, tastes great! Clean-living Billy Wright enjoys the skipper's privilege as he tries the champagne first in the dressing-room as Jesse Pye prepares to uncork another bottle.

Wolves' players and officials, with their womenfolk, are joined by friends of the club for a banquet at London's Cafe Royal to celebrate the winning of the 1949 FA Cup. The impetus of the success was maintained as a final placing of sixth that season was followed by a runners-up finish the following year. A spirited Cup defence ended in a fifth-round replay at Blackpool, though, after Plymouth and Sheffield United had been knocked out.

Have cases, will travel. Wolves' victorious 1949 squad, minus England duo Billy Wright and Johnny Hancocks, are captured in happy mood on the platform as they wait for their train to come in to whisk them on their way. From left are Angus McLean, Bill Crook, Lol Kelly, Bert Williams, Les Smith, Jimmy Stevenson, Sammy Smyth, Jesse Pye, Jimmy Dunn, Bill Shorthouse, Ray Chatham, Roy Pritchard and Jimmy Mullen.

The Fabulous Fifties

It wasn't just thrilling, attacking football and League Championship and FA Cup glory that packed 'em in on the terraces in Wolverhampton during the glorious post-war years. Molineux was also the stage for a busy 1949 public meeting that was addressed by Britain's most famous ever Prime Minister and well attended as a result. A platform was built in front of the old Waterloo Road Stand from which Winston Churchill could speak to the masses (above) and his words appeared to win the same sort of approval (below) that match-days did.

All dressed up and ready to go are Wolves' players and officials on their tour of South Africa in May and June of 1951. Clothing suppliers Cabanas, who ensured the party were immaculately turned out, arranged this photo opportunity in Johannesburg. The trip lasted almost a month and a half and brought the club 12 wins out of 12, including a 13-0 slaughter of Eastern Transvaal. Wolves returned to the republic in 1957.

Dawley-born Roy Pritchard, a fine stalwart of some 223 Wolves games, heads clear under the careful gaze of Bill Shorthouse in the 3-1 Division One triumph at Derby on August 29, 1951. A brace by Dennis Wilshaw and one goal from Jimmy Dunn - later to play for the Rams - gave Stan Cullis's side ample revenge for a 2-1 home defeat at the hands of Derby a week earlier but the season ended with a disappointing 16th position in the top division. Picture courtesy of Derby Evening Telegraph.

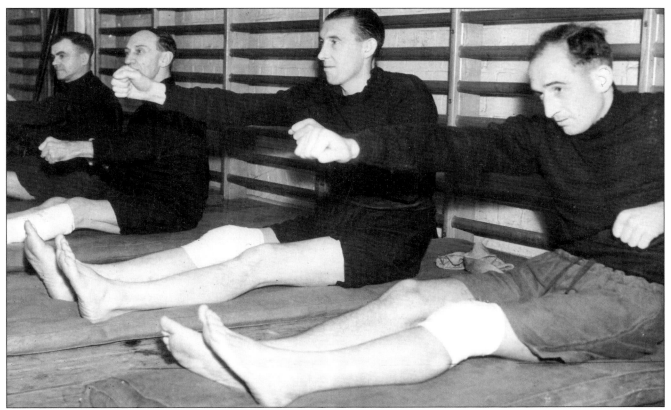

Tom Galley (second right) goes through rehabilitation at Patshull in October, 1951, following the ending of his career because of a knee injury. The Hednesford-born half-back, who also played in several other positions, served Wolves for more than 13 years from 1934, stacking up 204 League and FA Cup appearances and more than a further 70 in wartime football. He later played for both Grimsby, the club he had scored against in the 1939 FA Cup semi-final, and Kidderminster.

Beware! The year ends in one, so Tottenham's cockerel will be crowing loudly! Right-back John Short stretches but can't prevent this Spurs goal in Wolves' 4-2 First Division defeat at White Hart Lane on November 3, 1951. Roy Pritchard is on the far post and fellow defenders Bert Williams and Bill Shorthouse are pictured floundering in the six-yard area. At the time, the Londoners were staging an excellent defence of their League championship and were to finish runners-up.

FOREVER WOLVES

Dennis Wilshaw is shut out in this skirmish near the Aston Villa line in the 1951 Boxing Day derby at Molineux. Wolves lost 2-1 in front of more than 50,000, having drawn 3-3 the previous day at a Villa Park populated by 49,525. Christmas Day football may be unheard of now but Wolves fulfilled League fixtures on that date in four of the first six post-war seasons and continued to do so spasmodically until 1956-57.

Stoke keeper Dennis Herod thrusts out a hand but can't stop Jimmy Mullen scoring one of the goals by which Wolves won this Staffordshire derby 3-0 on March 8, 1952. Mullen's fellow winger Johnny Hancocks netted the other two for a side who had drawn 11 of their previous 17 League games but lost 1-0 at the Victoria Ground in October. The Wolves player closest to the ball is the prolific Roy Swinbourne.

Wolves were glimpsing greatness by the time they destroyed Manchester United 6-2 in this First Division clash on October 4, 1952. Roy Swinbourne, albeit hidden by fellow scorer Jimmy Mullen, is pictured firing past keeper Reg Allen for one of the goals that made up the second of his seven hat-tricks for the club. Swinbourne scored 21 goals in 41 League appearances in the campaign and his side finished third in the table.

Hawthorns combat in front of 54,480 spectators as Roy Swinbourne has the ball taken off his head by Albion keeper Norman Heath on October 18, 1952. Dennis Wilshaw is the other Wolves player pictured in a tense 1-1 draw in which Les Smith fired the visitors into a first-half lead, only for George Lee to head the equaliser three minutes from time. The Baggies no 5 is Joe Kennedy, with Ray Barlow in the background.

Roy Swinbourne is beaten to the punch by Charlton's legendary keeper Sam Bartram during the Londoners' 2-1 League win at Molineux on January 3, 1953. The centre-forward, a product of the famous Wath Wanderers nursery in Yorkshire, scored in the game and topped the club's score-charts that season. Second to him was Dennis Wilshaw, who is pictured in the background and who netted 18 times in League and Cup.

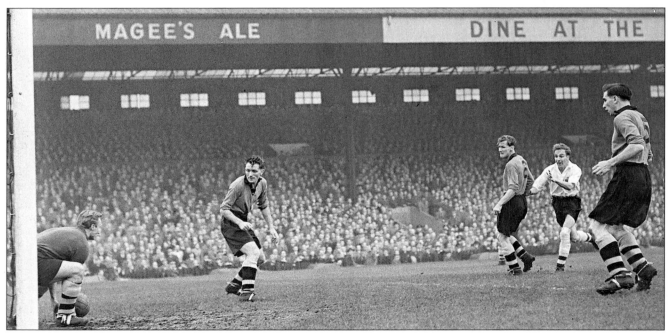

Burnden Park was rarely a happy hunting ground for Wolves over the years and this meeting with Bolton on October 24, 1953, brought them only a 1-1 draw despite their march towards the First Division title. Johnny Hancocks scored for Stan Cullis's side, who lost two of their first three matches and then went 18 unbeaten. Here, Bert Williams gathers safely from Harold Hassall, watched by (from left) Bill Guttridge, Bill Slater and no 5 Bill Shorthouse.

More festive rivalry between Wolves and Aston Villa as home keeper Keith Jones catches a Jimmy Mullen centre to frustrate the in-rushing Roy Swinbourne. Johnny Hancocks and Dennis Wilshaw scored the goals as the champions-elect gained revenge with a 2-1 Villa Park victory for a defeat by exactly the same score two days earlier on Christmas Eve, 1953. Wilshaw had also netted in the first meeting and scored in five successive matches in three weeks.

It's a winter wonderland for Wolves fans as their heroes skate to a thrilling 6-4 victory over Huddersfield on February 12, 1955. Dennis Wilshaw is beaten to the ball here by keeper Jack Wheeler but he was nevertheless on target twice and Johnny Hancocks three times, with Bill Slater the other scorer. Just to the right of Wilshaw is England international Bill McGarry - later to manage at Molineux. Wolves had lost 6-1 at Bolton a week earlier!

A familiar 1950s sight as Wolves, in front of the cameras and with their TV-friendly fluorescent shirts, take to the pitch (above) for a floodlit cracker against glamorous foreign opposition. Billy Wright, followed by Bill Shorthouse and Dennis Wilshaw, walks out in front of an expectant crowd before Moscow Spartak are destroyed 4-0 on November 16, 1954. The League champions hit four goals in the final 27 minutes through Dennis Wilshaw, Johnny Hancocks (2) and Roy Swinbourne. Below: Time to celebrate - with soft drinks, of course! From left are Shorthouse, Wright, Eddie Stuart, Hancocks, Ron Flowers, Swinbourne, Les Smith and Peter Broadbent.

A tremendous panorama view of Molineux, taken from near the back of the compact old North Bank terrace, captures the intoxicating scene at one of Wolves' famous floodlit friendlies in the 1950s. The matches drew enormous crowds to the stadium because of the novelty of winter night-time football and the opportunity for fans to see the best that Europe, and beyond, had to offer.

Dennis Wilshaw netted one of his four League and Cup hat-tricks for Wolves on the wintry day they recorded this 4-1 FA Cup round-five success over Charlton on February 19, 1955. Johnny Hancocks was also on target in a game sandwiched between spectacular League wins at home to Huddersfield (6-4) and Leicester (5-0) and at Manchester United (4-2). A snowy Bert Williams is seen putting paid to a Charlton excursion, covered by Bill Slater (left) and Eddie Stuart.

Wolves come under pressure during their FA Cup sixth-round exit at Roker Park on March 12, 1955. Bert Williams, capped 24 times by England, appeals for a free-kick as right-back Eddie Stuart, right-half Bill Slater and right-winger Johnny Hancocks look on from near the edge of the area. Sunderland won 2-0 but were beaten in the semi-final by Manchester City. Wolves went on to finish League runners-up to Chelsea. Picture courtesy of Newcastle Chronicle and Journal.

The game that did most to prevent Wolves from retaining the League championship. In front of a mind-blowing 75,043 at Stamford Bridge on Easter Saturday, 1955, Chelsea edged home 1-0 and the title was to be theirs as Wolves finished second. Here, Billy Wright handles on the line and concedes the 75th minute penalty from which Peter Sillett scored the winner. Bert Williams, Bill Shorthouse, a mainly-hidden Bill Slater, Ron Flowers and Chelsea no 9 Roy Bentley are also in view.

Proud ambassadors....Wolves' players are captured in relaxed, happy mood as they arrive for one of the two prestige friendlies on their trip to Russia in the summer of 1955. The club had been to Holland in 1948, Ireland in 1949 and South Africa in 1951, and were destined to carry on travelling far and wide. But it was a trail-blazing step at that time to venture behind the old Iron Curtain.

Ground-breaking in Russia in the summer of 1955

From left, Eddie Stuart, Ron Flowers, Nigel Sims, Roy Swinbourne, Bill Slater and Bert Williams are the men in shot as they wait for kick-off on a trip which brought disappointing results - a 3-0 beating against Moscow Spartak and a 3-2 defeat at the hands of Moscow Dynamo.

The backcloth is unmistakably East European as Wolves kick in prior to doing battle on Russian soil. Younger fans would now find it difficult to comprehend the importance that was attached both to these two tour games and the floodlit friendlies played at Molineux in the same era. National honour was at stake and the meeting of super-power teams from different countries paved the way for the launch of the European Cup.

It wasn't all work, no play in Moscow. Wolves players also had the chance to sightsee and were enthusiastic tourists. Pictured along with one or two of their hosts in this shot are (from left of the leading group) Bill Shorthouse, Billy Wright, Tommy McDonald, Joe Gardiner, Peter Broadbent, Nigel Sims and Scottish inside-forward Bobby Thomson.

Wolves were hailed as heroes when they took to the pitch ready for their game against Spartak. The formalities were at times prolonged and (from left) Bert Williams, Bill Slater, Ron Flowers, Colin Booth, Eddie Stuart, Roy Swinbourne, Peter Broadbent and Bill Shorthouse had to fight against impatience before getting ready for kick-off. The tour attracted what was then massive media interest, with Wolves carrying the torch for English football behind the Iron Curtain.

Wolves on the attack during their 3-0 defeat against Spartak as Colin Booth challenges the keeper while Roy Swinbourne takes a tumble to the left. The no 10 is Dennis Wilshaw. Pictured to the right nearer the stadium's distinctive Iron Curtain trappings is Peter Broadbent.

Lazing about on the Volga are this group of Wolves players and officials during the trip to Russia. Pictured are (from left) Colin Booth, Tommy McDonald, Scot Bobby Thomson, trainer Frank Morris, Dennis Wilshaw, Joe Baillie, Roy Swinbourne, a seated Bill Slater, coach Joe Gardiner and (nearest camera) Bert Williams. Thomson is not to be confused with the later full-back of the same name. This one was a forward, who scored in his one and only senior Wolves outing. A bespectacled Dr Richmond and journalist Alan Hoby (both standing to the right) are also pictured.

Back home off tour and Wolves were soon taking their frustrations out on Manchester City, whose keeper Bert Trautmann finds himself under pressure here from Peter Broadbent during the 7-2 thrashing at Molineux on August 27, 1955. Wolves had taken only one point from their opening two matches of the season but Roy Swinbourne (pictured left) scored four in this game, the also-pictured Colin Booth one and Johnny Hancocks two. In their next three games, Wolves beat Portsmouth 3-1, Cardiff 9-1 away and Huddersfield 4-0.

THE FABULOUS FIFTIES

Dennis Wilshaw moves in as a Moscow Dynamo defender clears his lines on November 9, 1955, during one of Wolves' most famous floodlit friendlies. The season after Moscow Spartak and Honved had been sent away defeated, goals by Bill Slater and Jimmy Mullen saw the League champions home 2-1 in front of a 55,480 gate against a side with Lev Yashin as their keeper. Wilshaw, a part-timer because of teaching duties, ended the season with 25 League and FA Cup goals.

Peter Broadbent stoops to head past Chelsea keeper Bill Robertson for Wolves' equaliser in a 3-2 victory at Stamford Bridge on February 4, 1956. The Londoners were title holders but this home defeat, containing further goals by Broadbent and Jimmy Murray, loosened their grip and Manchester United became champions. Wolves finished third, their own challenge undermined when Roy Swinbourne suffered the knee injury that brought about his premature retirement after an explosive start-of-season run of 17 goals in just 11 games.

Another happy day out in the capital for Wolves, who nevertheless had their hearts in their mouths when Charlton's Stuart Leary went down under a penalty-area challenge from Billy Wright. Goals by Jimmy Murray and Dennis Wilshaw did the trick in this 2-0 victory on March 24, 1956. Leary, who was also part of the Kent team who won cricket's county championship in 1970, spectacularly took his own life in 1988 by throwing himself off Cape Town's Table Mountain.

From a 1-1 League draw at Newcastle on October 26, 1957, champions-elect Wolves headed further north to Edinburgh for this 3-2 Monday night friendly win against Hibernian. Keeper Malcolm Finlayson is seen leaving his line in a hurry to collect from Joe Baker while Johannesburg-born Eddie Stuart is on hand in case of slips. Stuart, who bears a Scottish name, was once briefly linked with international honours north of the border because of his ancestry.

International Wolves

The dizzy 1954 heights of West Midlands football are epitomised by this England team picture before the game against West Germany in December of a year in which Wolves were the reigning League champions and Albion the FA Cup holders. Wolves are represented in the shot by Bert Williams, Bill Slater and Billy Wright while the Baggies have Joe Kennedy and Ronnie Allen. This is also one of the few photos showing Bill McGarry (then of Huddersfield) in international colours. Back row from left: Jimmy Trotter (trainer), Roger Byrne, Ron Staniforth, Bert Williams, Ray Wood, Len Phillips, Roy Bentley, Joe Kennedy. Front: Bill Slater, Stan Matthews, Len Shackleton, Billy Wright, Ronnie Allen, Tom Finney, Bill McGarry. England won 3-1 in this first clash of the nations since the war.

Skipper Billy Wright comforts a nervous-looking Bobby Charlton shortly before England depart for the 1958 World Cup in Sweden - one of Charlton's first flights since he survived the Munich air disaster. As if to confirm that Wolves were in a halcyon period, Molineux trio Bill Slater, Peter Broadbent and Eddie Clamp are seen near the top of the steps while Wolverhampton-born Don Howe is half-way up on the left. Next to Bobby Robson (light mac) is Brian Clough.

One of the few occasions the legendary Billy Wright actually got close to Ferenc Puskas during England's sobering visit to face Hungary in Budapest on May 23, 1954! The magical Magyars had won 6-3 at Wembley six months earlier and followed up with a 7-1 romp here. Wright, who soon became England centre-half after long service as their right-half, remained lifelong friends with his rival skipper Puskas and had revenge when the brilliant forward visited Molineux with Honved the following season.

Billy Wright is grounded and for once unable to help out as much-mourned Black Country boy Duncan Edwards boots clear from near the line in the England v Scotland international at Wembley on April 6, 1957. This 2-1 home victory, based on goals by Edwards and Albion's Derek Kevan, was England's first game since they had beaten Denmark 5-2 at Molineux on December 5 of the same season.

Dennis Wilshaw rises to nod home one of his four goals on the day England slammed the Scots 7-2 at Wembley. Wolves were also represented in this April 2, 1955, fixture by Bert Williams and skipper Billy Wright, Potteries-born Wilshaw playing 12 times for his country, including the 1954 World Cup in Switzerland, and emerging with the highly impressive record of ten goals. England's other scorers against the Scots were Nat Lofthouse (2) and Don Revie.

Characteristic agility from Bert Williams somehow helps avert a French goal from Bliard in England's friendly international in Paris on May 15, 1955. Although Williams, nicknamed The Cat, was beaten by a penalty that brought the game's only goal, it was a very proud day for Wolves. Ron Flowers and Billy Wright are seen at the left and right edges of the picture while Dennis Wilshaw was a fourth man from Molineux on view.

Roy Gratrix, Stanley Matthews and Billy Wright limber up at Roehampton on May 7, 1957, for England's World Cup qualifying game against the Republic of Ireland at Wembley the following night. Matthews and Wright were frequent rivals in matches between Blackpool and Wolves and played in the 5-1 slaughter of the Irish during a run of eight successive international wins. Gratrix, who was never capped, was with Blackpool. Picture courtesy of Blackpool Evening Gazette.

Peter Broadbent is pictured in his England colours, with Denis Law to the right of him, as he waits hopefully while Joe Baker challenges against Scotland at a packed Hampden Park on April 19, 1960. The Wolves inside-forward, winning the last of his seven senior caps, was out of luck and it took a Bobby Charlton penalty to earn the visitors a 1-1 draw. Ron Flowers was in the same team, having also been withdrawn from an important League game at Nottingham Forest the same weekend.

Hugh Curran swings his right foot and scores Scotland's goal in their 3-1 defeat by the auld enemy England at Wembley on May 22, 1971. Gordon Banks is the beaten keeper as the Wolves striker nets what proved to be his only goal from five caps at full international level. Curran went on to compile the impressive record of 47 goals and 98 senior appearances for Wolves before joining Oxford in September, 1972.

Bully for England! Steve Bull challenges Scotland's Dave McPherson in late May, 1989, on the extraordinary Hampden Park afternoon on which, as a player just out of the Third Division, he rifled in a tremendous late goal on his senior England debut. The striker had scored a magical 102 Wolves goals in the space of two seasons to earn the right to play alongside the likes of Tony Cottee (pictured centre) in Bobby Robson's line-up, who won 2-0.

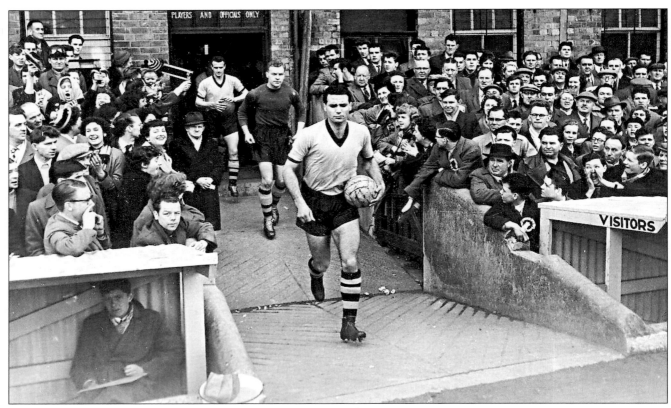

A sighten to quicken the hearts of all Molineux regulars......the emergence from the dressing-room of their Wolves heroes. Eddie Stuart leads the team out in this 1957-58 shot in one of Billy Wright's rare absences. Following the South African on to the pitch is Malcolm Finlayson, with Gerry Harris third in line. Stuart played 40 of the 42 games the club contested en route to becoming League champions for the second time.

Not this time! The brilliant Peter Broadbent scored the small matter of 145 goals in 497 first-team outings for Wolves but this effort in an FA Cup third-round tie at Lincoln in 1957-58 came to nothing. The inside-forward, who also played seven times for England, need not have worried, though. Jimmy Mullen netted the only goal of the tie against the Second Division side and his team went on to reach the sixth round as well as win the League title.

A picture to shoot down the theory that Stan Cullis never bothered with tactics! True, his style was one of direct attack-based football, with frequent use of quick wingers, but he has a captive audience here. The first-team party are all ears in a Molineux setting that had them donning their winter overcoats even if the Iron Man himself was warm enough in just his jacket!

Nimble-footed Wolves make light of the snow as they prepare at Aldersley Stadium for their FA Cup fourth-round tie against Portsmouth in January, 1958. Jimmy Mullen skips round the diving Malcolm Finlayson as Eddie Stuart looks on, with Peter Broadbent just behind him. To the left are Billy Wright and trainer Joe Gardiner. Wolves made short work of their task on match-day as well as they won 5-1 at Molineux and followed up with a 6-1 thrashing of Darlington in round five.

It's the end of the FA Cup road for Wolves as Bolton's Burnden Park again proves their graveyard. In this sixth-round tie on March 1, 1958, Dennis Stevens is pictured beating the flying Malcolm Finlayson to put the other Wanderers ahead, with Billy Wright and Eddie Stuart powerless to help. This defeat came in a run of six successive League wins for Wolves, Bolton going on to beat the tragic post-Munich Manchester United in the final. Picture courtesy of Bolton Evening News.

Champions again! Wolves' players appear in the Waterloo Road Stand to take their congratulations after their final home game of the 1957-58 campaign. Stan Cullis's side hit 103 League goals and clinched the title with this 2-0 victory over Preston on April 19. They followed up by thrashing Manchester United 4-0 at Old Trafford and would have equalled the then national record of 66 points in a season by winning their last match - but they lost 2-1 at Sheffield Wednesday.

Wolves headed off as Football League champions on tour of Switzerland and West Germany at the end of 1957-58 and stayed in the winning habit by beating Grasshoppers Zurich 4-1 on May 7 and Stuttgart 4-3 on May 10. Lining up alongside various officials in this warm-up for the following season's European Cup campaign are (from left) Malcolm Finlayson, Norman Deeley, George Showell, Joe Gardiner, Eddie Stuart, Colin Booth, Gerry Harris, Jimmy Mullen, Ron Flowers, Stan Cullis, John Ireland and Jim Marshall.

One for the family album. A bronzed Billy Wright is captured in happy pose with his wife Joy Beverley. In showbiz and sporting circles, they were very much the golden couple when they married in the summer of 1958 after a short courtship that was frequently interrupted by both his football with Wolves and England and her singing engagements with the Beverley Sisters. So dedicated was Wright to his career that he had barely had a girlfriend until their meeting when he was 34.

Wonderful Wolves launch their title defence with a 5-1 home victory over Nottingham Forest on the first day of 1958-59. A 52,656 crowd watch as Norman Deeley sidefoots the club's first goal into an empty net with keeper Chick Thomson getting back to his feet. Deeley was to work his wing magic brilliantly in the following eight months and finished the season with 19 goals in League and FA Cup. The main hero of kick-off day, though, was Bobby Mason, who hit a hat-trick.

Peter Broadbent and the ball are in Blackburn's net and Wolves are on their way to a 2-1 League win in front of a 43,209 Ewood Park crowd on September 13, 1958. The grounded Matt Woods has just turned in Norman Deeley's shot, the Rovers player also scoring an own goal for Wolves' winner at the venue the following year. The champions started 1958-59 with five wins from eight games and went on to retain their title.

Wolves were crowned champions for a second successive year on April 18, 1959, with Manchester United second, fully six points adrift. This game with Luton was only a few minutes old when Colin Booth beat defender Brendan McNally and scored with a header. Jimmy Murray (pictured), Peter Broadbent (2) and Eddie Clamp completed a 5-0 romp as Stan Cullis's side totalled more than 100 First Division goals for the second of four consecutive years.

Handy artwork sums up the Molineux mood as League champions Wolves beat FA Cup winners Nottingham Forest 3-1 to lift the Charity Shield in August, 1959. A bullet header by Jimmy Murray, watched by fellow scorer Micky Lill, is too good for centre-half Bob McKinlay and keeper Thompson. Peter Broadbent scored the other goal for rampant Wolves.

Wolves began their 1959-60 title defence with two wins, the second of them this 3-1 midweek victory over Sheffield Wednesday. No 9 Jimmy Murray scored this and one of the other goals, Eddie Clamp getting the other. Micky Lill is the Wolves player following the ball in while the no 5 is Peter Swan, who played 19 times for England but was jailed following football's match-fixing investigation of 1963.

FOREVER WOLVES

An early Sheffield Wednesday reunion for Wolves as Jimmy Murray tries a flying header on September 2 - a night he scored twice more. His heroics earned only a 2-2 draw but the Dover-born forward was to end 1959-60 with a tremendous tally of 34, all but five in the League. All told, he scored 166 times in 299 senior Wolves appearances, won two League championship medals and an FA Cup winner's medal, and represented England under-23s and the Football League.

Three days after Hillsborough, Wolves went goal-crazy at Maine Road. Manchester City led 2-0 after seven minutes and must have thought scoring four would earn at least a point. But Stan Cullis's side rattled in six in an astonishing game! Murray (left), later to join City, and Bill Slater (right) led the way with two apiece, Micky Lill got one and Norman Deeley netted with this close-range shot. It was at Maine Road, coincidentally, that Wolves were to lose the title in the following spring when Burnley won there in the final fixture.

Following the blip of a defeat at Fulham, Wolves returned to goal-scoring and winning form by beating Blackburn 3-1 on September 12, 1959. Norman Deeley's powerful header provided no 2 and made for miserable viewing for covering defender Ken Taylor (left). Deeley, from Wednesbury, ended the season with 19 goals, including two in the FA Cup final against these same opponents.

A jolt for the champions. Wolves followed up a 9-0 midweek slaughter of Fulham by losing 3-1 at Blackpool on September 19, 1959. Neither centre-half George Showell, replacement for the great and by-then-retired Billy Wright, nor keeper Malcolm Finlayson can do anything to stop this header from Jackie Mudie. Wolves often had problems at compact Bloomfield Road and Mudie took full advantage on this occasion with a first-half hat-trick.

FOREVER WOLVES

A massive 59,344 crowd roared super Spurs to a 5-1 victory on October 10, 1959 - just a week after Wolves had beaten Luton by the same score. Tottenham threaten here with a header that left-back Gerry Harris covers on the line. Terry Medwin raises his arm in anticipation while no 6 Eddie Clamp, Eddie Stuart and the grounded Malcolm Finlayson are the other Wolves men in shot.

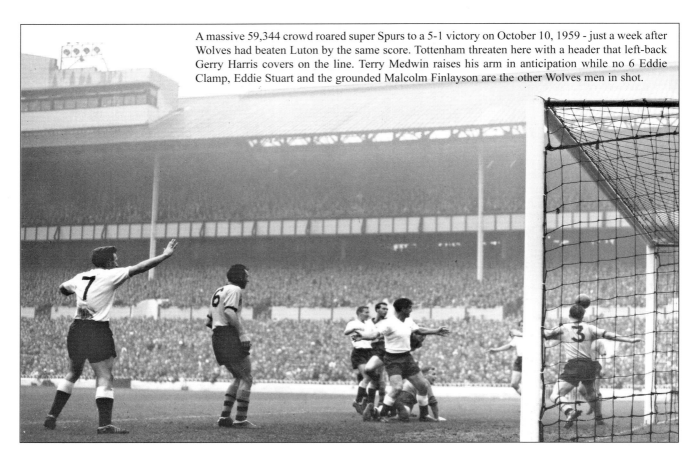

Bobby Mason is thwarted on the Halloween afternoon in 1959 that Wolves beat Newcastle 2-0 at Molineux. Jimmy Murray is lending support and was to get his name on the score-sheet, along with Peter Broadbent. The Newcastle defender standing patrol is Bob Stokoe, Sunderland's FA Cup winning manager in 1973.

John Kirkham made his League debut on the mid-October day in 1959 that Wolves edged to a 3-2 win at home to Manchester United. Jimmy Murray scored twice, one of them with this tremendous diving header. The United keeper is Harry Gregg, one of the heroes of the Munich air crash 18 months earlier, while Wilf McGuinness (under the ball) and Bill Foulkes are the defenders to the right.

A familiar sight for travelling Wolves fans in the autumn of 1959. John Dick drives past Malcolm Finlayson to open the scoring for West Ham at Upton Park on November 21. Stan Cullis's side responded with goals by Peter Broadbent and Tipton-born Bobby Mason but suffered a fourth successive away League defeat in a run broken by victory at Albion on December 5. Eddie Clamp is the player challenging the scorer and Phil Woosnam the West Ham man in the background.

Arsenal 4 Wolves 4 - and this could have been a winner for the visitors! No 10 Peter Broadbent is denied by a free-kick decision by the referee as he despatches the ball into the Gunners net on January 2, 1960. Bobby Mason, on target along with Eddie Clamp, Jimmy Murray and Des Horne, is the other Wolves player in the picture while the home keeper is Jim Standen, later of West Ham. Stan Cullis's side had lost two of their previous three matches, two of them against Bolton.

A flurry of snow is kicked up in front of the expectant North Bank as Norman Deeley leaves Newcastle duo McMichael and Bell in his wake and scores one of the goals in Wolves' 4-2 FA Cup third-round replay win. Ron Flowers, Jimmy Murray and Des Horne notched the others in a highly prolific spell for the club, who had drawn 4-4 at Arsenal on January 2 and were to beat Manchester City 4-2 in the League at Molineux shortly afterwards.

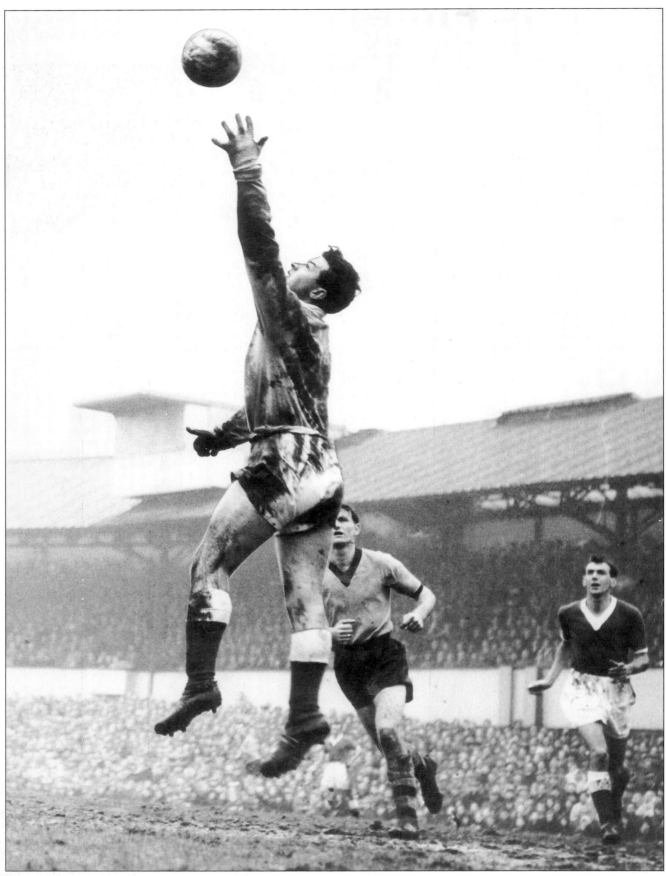

The in-rushing Jimmy Murray is denied by keeper Willie Duff's rise from the Molineux mud in an attack at the North Bank end - but Wolves weren't to be denied. They edged home 2-1 in this FA Cup fourth-round tie against Charlton on January 30, 1960, thanks to goals by Peter Broadbent and Des Horne, and were starting to think about Wembley. The feeling grew when they won 4-1 at Luton and 2-1 at Leicester in the following two rounds.

Wolves made it two victories over Luton in the space of four days when they defeated them 3-2 in this First Division game at Molineux on February 23, 1960. The previous Saturday, they had beaten the Hatters 4-1 in the FA Cup at Kenilworth Road. Peter Broadbent didn't get on the score-sheet in that fifth-round tie but is pictured making his scoring mark in the follow-up, in which Jimmy Murray and Des Horne were also on the mark. Luton were relegated that season.

Aston Villa's ex-Wolves keeper Nigel Sims hangs on and appears to be winning a free-kick for a challenge by Peter Broadbent during the all-West Midlands FA Cup semi-final at The Hawthorns on March 26, 1960. Match-winner Norman Deeley is lurking in the background during a tie which was won 1-0, watched by 55,596 and followed by three successive Wolves victories in the League, the first of them 6-1 at home to title rivals Burnley.

No mistake from keeper Malcolm Finlayson as he takes the ball safely under pressure from Don Revie during Wolves' 3-0 First Division victory at Leeds on April 2, 1960. Bill Slater and George Showell are the covering defenders on a day when Gerry Mannion's hat-trick was the difference between the teams. Leeds were to be relegated a few weeks later and spend the next four seasons in the Second Division while Wolves went close to making it a hat-trick of successive League Championship triumphs.

Goal-hungry Jimmy Murray cracks a shot against the legs of Nottingham Forest's Tony Barton - the man who was to lead Aston Villa to European Cup glory in 1982 - as Wolves step up their bid for a League and FA Cup double in the spring of 1960. The forward scored twice in a 3-1 Easter Monday First Division win on April 18 and has Ron Flowers in support in this raid. Wolves were on course for another championship triumph following their successes of 1957-58 and 1958-59.

A let-off for Wolves in their East Midlands v West Midlands derby at the City Ground the following day on April 19, 1960. Malcolm Finlayson dives, fails to reach a penalty by Jim Iley that was conceded by Gerry Harris and is relieved to see it flash wide of his post. The 0-0 draw with Nottingham Forest came on Easter Tuesday and was only of partial help to Stan Cullis's side of title-chasers.

A resounding 5-1 win at Chelsea kept Wolves top of Division One on the last Saturday of 1959-60. They then had 54 points, one more than both Spurs and Burnley. Unfortunately, Burnley, having drawn 0-0 at home to Fulham, still had to visit Manchester City in a game postponed from FA Cup quarter-final day. They won and so denied the Cullis Machine a third successive title. Here, Peter Sillett handles a Peter Broadbent shot and gives Wolves a penalty Ron Flowers converted. Also pictured are (from left) Reg Matthews, goalscorer Jimmy Murray and Sylvan Anderton.

FA Cup Final 1960

A job fit for a civic dignitary.....Mayor of Wolverhampton Alderman Mr Norman Bagley helps Wolves officials, including long-serving secretary Jack Howley (right), with the ballot to distribute tickets for Wolves' FA Cup final against Blackburn in 1960. His assistance was required after 31,907 applications had been received for the 8,500 tickets still available once season ticket holders had been accommodated.

May the best team win! Bill Slater, successor to Billy Wright as Wolves skipper and centre-half, greets his Blackburn counterpart Ronnie Clayton before the FA Cup final on May 7, 1960. Stan Cullis's side had beaten Newcastle (in a Molineux replay), Charlton, Luton, Leicester and Aston Villa on their goal-filled route to Wembley. The referee is Mr K Howley (Middlesbrough).

Not this time! Norman Deeley, the two-goal hero of Wolves' 3-0 Wembley triumph, races in but finds nothing doing for him on this occasion as Blackburn keeper Harry Leyland takes off spectacularly high to his left.

Peter Dobing looks on admiringly as Malcolm Finlayson goes down to save well in a Blackburn attack. George Showell is the nearest covering defender.

Mick McGrath, who opened the scoring with an own goal, emerges with the ball as his Blackburn team-mate Ronnie Clayton and Wolves' Peter Broadbent go down in a heap. Rovers were themselves in some disarray after centre-forward Derek Dougan - later to serve Wolves on and off the field - had gone into action in the final despite sensationally handing in a transfer request the previous day.

SOUVENIR EDITION
Sporting Star
Vauxhall for Value Don Everall for Vauxhalls
for GLAZING EDWARDS CLEVELAND STREET Wolverhampton
May 7th
No. 4725 Telephone 23333 WOLVERHAMPTON, SATURDAY, MAY 7, 1960 PRICE 2½d.

OURS 🏆 AGAIN

WOLVES 3, BLACKBURN 0 — Attendance 100,000 ; Receipts £49,816 — THE TWO IN ONE PICTURE

* The 1960 version of the Sporting Star's famous headlines immortalising Wolves' FA Cup heroics.

Would that be tea you're drinking, sir, or something a little stronger? Wolves skipper Bill Slater refuses to be separated from the FA Cup as he toasts victory. Slater had played as an amateur for Blackpool in the 1951 final and, as well as appearing 12 times for England, represented Great Britain in the 1952 Olympic Games. His golden 1959-60 campaign led to him being named Footballer of the Year.

The happy homecoming! Tens of thousands of fans line the streets near Wolverhampton's town centre for a glimpse of the silverware and the triumphant Wanderers players. Note the photographers perched on precarious ledges to capture the action. It was Wolves' first FA Cup triumph for 11 years. Little did everyone know it would be their last for well over 40 seasons to the present day.

Mere Mortals Again

Action from Wolves' last appearance in the Charity Shield as keeper Geoff Sidebottom dives bravely at the feet of Burnley and England forward Ray Pointer, with Eddie Stuart as cover close by. The other four visiting players in the picture are (from left) John Kirkham, Jimmy Murray, Barry Stobart and Eddie Clamp. Wolves' goals in a 2-2 draw at Turf Moor came from Murray and Norman Deeley.

Wolves return to Stamford Bridge for their second away game of 1960-61 and Geoff Sidebottom, who played most of the first half of the season in place of Malcolm Finlayson, dives to push aside this shot from Charlie Livesey as Gerry Harris looks on. The lurking Chelsea player is Jimmy Greaves, who hit a hat-trick on a day Jimmy Murray (2) and Des Horne scored at the other end in a 3-3 draw.

Up goes Blackpool's England keeper Tony Waiters as he finds himself under pressure from the leaping Ron Flowers in his side's single-goal defeat at Molineux on September 3, 1960. Wolves, who also have Jimmy Murray and no 10 Peter Broadbent on hand, had Bobby Mason on target as they made it four wins and a draw from their first five matches of the season. They won again at home to Leicester four days later.

Wolves' first defeat of 1960-61 came on September 10 in this sunny encounter at Goodison, where Brian Harris sticks out a leg to dispossess Jimmy Murray - scorer of another 25 goals in that season. Eddie Clamp peers for a view of the action while Wolves scorer Ron Flowers is partly to be seen behind Everton's Jimmy Gabriel. Stan Cullis's side took revenge over the Toffees by beating them 4-1 back at Molineux in the January.

MERE MORTALS AGAIN

A young Ted Farmer showed the way to goal when he scored twice in Wolves' 3-1 victory at Manchester United on September 24, 1960. Des Horne also netted but, at the other end, Dennis Viollet demonstrated how not to finish as he put this sitter over the bar with Geoff Sidebottom out of his goal. The game was one of Wolves' five successive victories over United from 1959 to 1961, three of them at Old Trafford.

Ted Farmer again shows his mettle as he tucks away one of Wolves' goals in their enthralling 4-4 draw at Newcastle on October 15, 1960. Peter Broadbent (2) and Jimmy Murray were also on the score-sheet at a time when Stan Cullis's side had won only once in eight matches. Three days earlier, they had lost 2-0 away to FK Austria in their first-ever European Cup Winners' Cup game - a deficit they were to turn around spectacularly in the second leg by winning 5-0.

Ron Flowers has his head in his hands - but he didn't need to. Bobby Mason has just scored one of the goals in Wolves' astonishing 5-5 Molineux draw with Tfilis Dynamo on November 10, 1960, in one of the last of the club's prestige friendlies. The FA Cup holders were at the time in between the two legs of their European Cup Winners Cup tie with FK Austria.

Peter Broadbent threads a shot through the Turf Moor mud for one of Wolves' goals in the scoring feast with Burnley on November 12, 1960. Ted Farmer, hidden nearer the camera, netted twice but Stan Cullis's side lost 5-3, having beaten Nottingham Forest at Molineux the week before by the same score. Wolves were to finish third and Burnley, in their title defence, one place and six points behind.

Denis Law is the Manchester City player closing in hungrily between Bill Slater (left) and Eddie Clamp as Geoff Sidebottom pounces on a loose ball in this Maine Road clash on December 10, 1960. Wolves ran out 4-2 victors, with four different scorers, at a time when goals were flowing very freely. It was the club's seventh win in eight League games in a run that had seen them find the opposition net no fewer than 29 times.

Not all that it appears! It may look like a Wolves goal, given the gesture of Claverley-born left-back Gerry Harris, veteran of 270 senior appearances for the club. But it's West Ham who are about to celebrate as Malcolm Musgrove falls after heading past Geoff Sidebottom for the opener in a crushing 5-0 home win at Upton Park on December 17. The other Wolves face to be seen is that of Johnny Kirkham.

Another Villa v Wolves festive occasion as ex-Molineux keeper Nigel Sims pushes away a cross-shot and denies the in-rushing Jimmy Murray (left) and Ted Farmer. Vic Crowe is the left one of the two Villa defenders. Wolves won this Christmas Eve clash 2-0, triumphed 3-2 in the return on Boxing Day and Farmer totalled three goals over the double-header as part of a best-in-the-club season's haul of 28.

Get in! Jimmy Murray crashes home one of the goals against Chelsea on New Year's Eve, 1960, that made up the last of his five hat-tricks for Wolves. John Kirkham, Ted Farmer and Cliff Durandt also netted in the 6-1 thrashing of the Londoners, who became Stan Cullis's side's third victims in a run of five consecutive First Division victories in mid-season. The teams had earlier drawn 3-3 at Stamford Bridge, Murray scoring twice.

Up go the heads during Wolves' goalless draw at Sheffield Wednesday on March 11, 1961. Ron Flowers fails to get airborne at the near post but Tom McAnearney nods behind for a corner while team-mate Peter Johnson offers him close support. It was the first time the championship challengers had failed to score in 14 League and FA Cup matches but they made amends as they hit five against visiting Birmingham a week later.

Another meeting of great minds in the Molineux tunnel area as Stan Cullis and Billy Wright are reunited well after the end of the latter's playing career. Leaning against the wall behind them are Fred Goodwin (left) and Alan Hinton, both of whom were to make their League debuts for the club in 1961-62. Goodwin, not to be confused with the early-1970s Birmingham manager of the same name, went on to make 47 senior Wolves appearances and Hinton won League championship honours with Brian Clough's Derby in the 1970s.

Ted Farmer leaves Manchester City's Bill Leivers in his wake but fails to score in his final appearance of a tremendous 1960-61 debut season. The 1-0 April Fool's Day home win was marked by bad feeling, Farmer incurring the wrath of the City camp when he stood over the fallen body of keeper Bert Trautmann in exaggerated applause of Jimmy Murray's winning goal. Wolves, beaten 3-1 by Rangers in the semi-final of the Cup Winners Cup, finished third in the table and passed 100 League goals for the fourth successive season.

Gerry Harris and Malcolm Finlayson watch a Leicester effort clear the bar during Wolves' 3-0 beating at Filbert Street on November 4, 1961. It was a third defeat in four games for the club, who had kicked off the season with only one win in eight matches. Scottish-born Finlayson was nearing the end of his stint as first-choice keeper at Molineux, having collected two League Championship medals and an FA Cup winner's medal following his arrival from Millwall.

The dependable Jimmy Murray tries an early header at the Fulham goal at Craven Cottage on December 2, 1961 - the day he was to score the only goal of the game and one of his 17 that season. Fellow forward Ted Farmer is also seen challenging the Londoners' defence while the player farthest to the right is midfielder Alan Mullery, later of Tottenham, England and Fulham again.

Yet more of Jimmy Murray, this time posing problems in the Carlisle defence as the Fourth Division club are ousted from the FA Cup 3-1 in this rearranged third-round game at Molineux on January 8, 1962. Terry Wharton (2) and Peter Broadbent scored in a tie that was originally postponed because of snow but Wolves were beaten 2-1 by visiting Albion in the next round. The visit of the Cumbrians brought Stan Cullis's side their only win in a seven-game stretch in the middle section of a disappointing season.

Wolves caved in embarrassingly when they were hammered 7-2 at Blackpool on January 20, 1962. Here, South African Peter Hauser sticks out a foot to beat Malcolm Finlayson, who made way for Fred Davies to go in for his debut the following week. Eddie Stuart and George Showell are the helpless defenders, with Ray Charnley the other Blackpool attacker. Stan Cullis's side won their next three League games but still finished only 18th in the table.

Another new dawn for Ted Farmer as the yesteryear Steve Bull scores the last of his four goals in the 8-1 slaughter of Manchester City on the opening day of 1962-63. Wolves were subsequently robbed of a potential superstar, with Farmer chopped down in his prime after rattling in 44 goals in only 62 games. The other Wolves players are Jimmy Murray and home debutant Fred Goodwin. The City man behind the referee is a young David Wagstaffe, who scored their goal.

Ted Farmer turns in Wolves' second equaliser in their 4-2 home win over Blackburn on September 1, 1962. Alan Hinton (far background) netted a brace that day and went on to top the club's goal list with 19 for the season. Wolves won six of their first seven League matches and piled on the agony for the two covering Rovers players pictured. Mick McGrath (standing) scored an own goal in the 1960 FA Cup final meeting of the clubs, in which the sliding Matt Woods also played.

Wolves and Honved were reunited on December 3, 1962, for a Molineux friendly bearing echoes of their famous 1954 meeting. Keeper Farago was the hero of the night and punches clear from Jimmy Murray in a game in which Alan Hinton's second-half goal secured a 1-1 draw. Wednesbury-born left-winger Hinton, later to win the League Championship with Brian Clough's Derby, made 78 League and Cup appearances for Wolves, scoring 29 times.

FOREVER WOLVES

Albion thought they had escaped when this snow-hit West Midlands derby at Molineux on Boxing Day, 1962, was abandoned at half-time with Wolves 2-0 ahead. Their relief was relatively short-lived, though, as they were hammered 7-0 in the rearranged game nearly three months later! Peter Broadbent (left) and Barry Stobart are the attackers in this aerial ballet also involving Wolverhampton-born Don Howe (left) and Chuck Drury.

Later in the severe winter of 1962-63, Wolves and Sheffield United went slip-sliding to a 0-0 draw at Molineux on January 19 in front of only 10,484 shivering fans - the only League game Wanderers played that month. Keeper Fred Davies and right-back Bobby Thomson, who was born in Smethwick and played eight times for England as well as exactly 300 times for Wolves, repel a header from the grounded Derek Pace.

MERE MORTALS AGAIN

Terry Wharton opens the scoring in Wolves' thrilling 4-3 victory at Birmingham on March 9, 1963. John Kirkham, Peter Broadbent and Barry Stobart scored the other goals in this first win in six games - a result which exacted some revenge for Blues' 2-0 triumph at Molineux in the autumn.

It's the Black Country re-match against Albion on March 16, 1963, and a resounding 7-0 Wolves win. Here, Barry Stobart lets fly to score the second goal from a pass by Peter Broadbent (left). Stobart and Alan Hinton each netted twice and Terry Wharton three times. The Albion men pictured are (from left) keeper Tony Millington, Graham Williams, Bobby Cram, Stan Jones, Ron Bradley and Don Howe.

Only two minutes were on the clock when Barry Stobart took off for this acrobatic header that flew past keeper Mike Pinner and into the Leyton Orient net on March 30, 1963. Pinner, an amateur, played against Wolves five times - each game with a different club and each ending in defeat! Despite the early goal, it was not easy for Wolves, who ground out a 2-1 victory in which Terry Wharton also scored.

Barry Stobart, later to play for Aston Villa, climbs well to win a header during Wolves' 3-1 home win over the Second City club on Easter Monday, 1963. Terry Wharton, Jimmy Murray and Alan Hinton scored for Wolves, who won 2-0 at Villa the following day during a crazy April in which they had to cram in nine games in 28 days after snow and frost had played havoc with the winter programme. Villa's players are (from left) John Sleewenhoek, Alan Deakin, Mike Tindall and Charlie Aitken.

Wolves are denied by a goalline clearance by Jim Langley in their home clash with Fulham on April 27, 1963, although they still took the points 2-1 thanks to goals by Ron Flowers and Alan Hinton. Jimmy Murray and Terry Wharton are the forwards closing in while Bobby Robson is the Fulham man on the far right and Alan Mullery the other player lending close support to keeper Tony Macedo. Wharton was in a purple patch, having scored ten times in ten games shortly before and eventually finishing the season with 16 goals.

Safe catch by Fred Davies - but he was beaten twice as Wolves lost 2-0 against Nottingham Forest at the City Ground on April 30, 1963. Gerry Harris (left), a half-hidden Bobby Thomson and Dave Woodfield are also pictured from a side who had lost at Manchester United eight days earlier and who lost their final three away matches of the season. They had also lost 4-3 at Forest in the third round of the FA Cup.

If there aren't enough hours in the working day to finish everything, then just get the board and counters out in front of the fireside and put the finishing touches to those tactics for the weekend! Stan Cullis demonstrates that being manager of Wolves isn't just about the dressing-room, the training ground and the bench as he devises his plans. The club finished fifth in the First Division in 1962-63 in what was their last good season under Cullis.

Roger Hunt, a member of England's victorious 1966 World Cup final team, is denied by Fred Davies in Liverpool's 3-1 victory at Molineux on September 9, 1963. Peter Broadbent and Dave Woodfield are the players chasing back, with Ron Flowers and Chris Crowe in the background. Flowers scored but his side were in an unhappy run of five consecutive defeats which included a thumping at Anfield a week later. Picture courtesy of Liverpool Post and Echo.

Malcolm Finlayson's glorious Molineux career, containing two League Championship triumphs and FA Cup success, ended ingloriously in this game at Liverpool on September 16, 1963. Two days after a 5-1 thrashing at home to Blackburn, Finlayson came in at Anfield for what proved his only appearance of the season - and Wolves lost 6-0. Gerry Harris and Ron Flowers are the onlookers, with Jimmy Melia - later of Wolves - in between them.

Ray Crawford was given the honour of the captaincy when he returned to Ipswich with Wolves for this game on April 14, 1964. Crawford, capped twice by England, is still the East Anglians' all-time top scorer and was given a warm reception when he went to toss up with home skipper Bill Baxter. Wolves lost 1-0 and finished a mediocre 16th in Stan Cullis's last full season, although their two remaining games after this brought 4-0 wins at home to Fulham and away to Bolton. Within a few more months, the most famous manager in the club's history had gone. Picture courtesy of Ipswich Evening Star.

Farewell to Cullis

A downcast Stan Cullis leaves Molineux for the last time as an employee of Wolverhampton Wanderers following the dismissal that stunned the club's supporters on September 15, 1964. Shortly before, he had returned to work following several weeks' illness and so sensitive were the Express & Star about the departure of a man revered so greatly in the town and the game that they wrote only of his 'departure,' not once using the word 'sacking' in the paper's extensive coverage. As a magnificent centre-half, the Ellesmere Port-born son of a Wulfrunian played 171 games for the club in League and FA Cup and plenty more in wartime football. He then managed the club for 16 years, during which he won the League Championship three times, the FA Cup twice and the Charity Shield.

Gloom following the exit of Wolves' greatest-ever manager still hung over Molineux when Manchester United visited on October 17, 1964. The club lost four League games out of four straight afterwards, including a 5-1 hiding at Albion. United, on course to win the title, took no mercy on a side now managed by Andy Beattie as they won 4-2, defender Gerry Harris turning in John Connelly's cross here for an own goal. Fred Davies and Denis Law are the men in closest attendance.

Merseyside was no happy hunting ground for Wolves just before and just after Stan Cullis's departure. This trip to Goodison Park on December 5, 1964 - Bobby Thomson's 21st birthday - brought a resounding 5-0 defeat despite a header off the line by Gerry Harris. From the left, Hugh McIlmoyle, Dave Woodfield, Everton's Fred Pickering, Terry Wharton and Liverpudlian Fred Davies are the players looking on. Wolves players are wearing black arm-bands following the death of director Cliff Everall the day before. Picture courtesy of Liverpool Post and Echo.

Scot Andy Beattie had been in charge for more than a couple of months by the time Wolves went to Stamford Bridge on December 12, 1964, and suffered a 2-1 defeat despite a Ray Crawford goal. No fewer than 28 players were used in that season - the club's highest total for almost 30 years - but relegation still came to Molineux for the first time since 1923. Here, Dave Woodfield (left) and Fred Davies are powerless as Barry Bridges glances in the Londoners' first goal.

Another trip to London, another defeat. Arsenal proved too strong for Wolves in the first game of 1965, winning 4-1 at Highbury despite a goal from the pictured Ray Crawford, who was on his way to being the club's top marksman for the season with 15 in League and FA Cup. Tony Burns is the Gunners keeper, Frank McLintock is in the background and no 2 is Wolverhampton-born Don Howe, who always regretted missing out on joining the Molineux staff.

Bobby Thomson sweeps the ball away from danger as Roger Hunt closes in menacingly during Wolves' 2-1 defeat at Liverpool on February 13, 1965. The three visiting players in the background are (from left) Ken Knighton, Bobby Woodruff and Johnny Kirkham. Woodruff scored for a Wolves side who were to include a 7-4 defeat at Tottenham shortly afterwards in a tale of away-day woe that season. Picture courtesy of Liverpool Post and Echo.

FAREWELL TO CULLIS

Bobby Woodruff celebrates a goal from Paddy Buckley's pull-back but relegation was close when Wolves lost 4-2 at home to Everton on April 17, 1965. Brian Labone, Tommy Wright and Gordon West are the defenders watching the ball go in during an Easter Saturday clash that put one of the final nails in the coffin. Wolves had played more than 1,380 games in 33 years' continuous membership of the top flight. Picture courtesy of Liverpool Post and Echo.

The last rites…..Aston Villa's 1-0 home win over Leicester on April 20 finally confirmed the big drop at Molineux, although Wolves beat Sunderland 3-0 there on the same day thanks to a hat-trick of Bobby Woodruff headers. After top-six finishes in 17 out of 26 seasons, relegation hit the club hard and only 13,839 fans watched the last game at home to Liverpool. The Merseysiders won 3-1 despite making ten changes as they rested players for the FA Cup final against Leeds five days later. Here, Hugh McIlmoyle threatens one of Liverpool's four debutants on the night, appropriately-named keeper Bill Molyneux. Picture courtesy of Liverpool Post and Echo.

Full-back Bobby Thomson, backed up by the mercurial Peter Knowles, pushes forward into attack as Wolves - now in a revolutionary all gold strip - turn the screw against visiting Rotherham in the eighth game of their 1965-66 Second Division season. Knowles got on the score-sheet as a 4-1 win spelled revenge following the Millers' 4-3 triumph at Millmoor six days earlier but this game was a watershed for Andy Beattie. The Scot was sacked after the 9-3 defeat at Southampton five days later on September 18.

Dave MacLaren is watched by his central defenders John Holsgrove and Dave Woodfield and his on-the-line full-back Joe Wilson as he pushes a corner behind during the 2-1 defeat at Carlisle on February 5, 1966. Wolves, beaten the previous week by their then jinx club Coventry, lost only one of their next ten games after this trip to Brunton Park but still finished only sixth in Division Two in the days when promotion play-offs hadn't even been thought of. Picture courtesy of Carlisle Evening News.

Bouncing Back

Carlisle is again the venue, this time in 1966-67, and the promotion omens weren't good for Wolves when they headed for Brunton Park on September 10. Ronnie Allen's side had lost their opening two games of 1966-67 but this 3-1 win heralded a change of fortunes that continued with huge wins over Blackburn (4-0) and Cardiff (7-1) in the following two League matches. Fred Davies is the keeper on his toes as Dave Woodfield fails to cut out a shot that John Holsgrove (no 6) and Bobby Thomson (no 3) are ready for. Hugh McIlmoyle, who served Carlisle before and after his spell at Molineux, is the Wolves player to the left. Picture courtesy of Carlisle Evening News.

White-shirted John Holsgrove is thwarted by keeper David Best during the FA Cup third-round tie at Third Division Oldham on January 28, 1967. Wolves were two down with two minutes to go and many of their fans were on their way out of the ground when their side pulled one back. Some then re-entered, just in time to see the equaliser! Bobby Thomson and Mike Bailey scored in the 2-2 draw and Wolves won the replay 4-1. Picture courtesy of Oldham Evening Chronicle.

What an introduction! Derek Dougan steers in the goal that gave him a hat-trick against Hull on his home debut for Wolves on March 25, 1967. More than 30,000 were at Molineux to see a 4-0 win that was the sixth of eight successive victories for Ronnie Allen's team. Dougan, who had previously played for Portsmouth, Blackburn, Aston Villa, Peterborough and Leicester, had made his debut at Plymouth a week before. He scored nine goals in only 11 Wolves games that season.

Wolves made it a victorious top-flight return when they went to Fulham on August 19, 1967, and won 2-1 with goals by Mike Bailey and Derek Dougan. Unheard of today, they made the step-up without any big signings, the inclusion of the available-again Bailey for Graham Hawkins being the only change from the final match of 1966-67 at Crystal Palace. Here, John Holsgrove robs striker Steve Earle, with Dave Burnside in the background. Picture courtesy of Ken Coton.

A cruel twist for Wolves on their visit to Anfield on November 25, 1967. Evan Williams, the Scot with a Welsh name and later to play for Celtic, saves an 83rd minute penalty from Tommy Smith with the score at 1-1. But a retake was ordered and Willie Stevenson drove home to give Liverpool a 2-1 win. Alun Evans had equalised for Wolves just after half-time against the club he was to join less than a year later. Picture courtesy of Liverpool Post and Echo.

John Holsgrove (no 6) deflects a Roger Hunt shot narrowly wide in the return clash with Liverpool on March 2, 1968 - a 1-1 Molineux draw. Also pictured in this all-star cast are (from left) Bobby Thomson, Peter Knowles, Emlyn Hughes (later to skipper Wolves), Mike Bailey and Dave Woodfield. Derek Dougan scored for a Wolves side who kept their heads above water to finish 17th in their first season back in the top flight. Picture courtesy of Liverpool Post and Echo.

Phil Parkes makes a sartorial change as he sports the keeper's number one on his front for the opening game of the 1968-69 season at Ipswich. It was an idea brought back that close season from America, where Ronnie Allen's side spent over a month and a half winning a summer tournament as Los Angeles Wolves and where TV bosses had players wearing their numbers on their fronts to make them more recognisable. John Holsgrove, watched by Dave Woodfield, Derek Parkin and John O'Rourke, clears here in the 1-0 defeat at Portman Road, the outfield Wolves men having not followed an identification experiment Parkes continued for several weeks. Picture courtesy of Ipswich Evening Star.

Alun Evans wasted no time enhancing his reputation as Britain's costliest teenager when he returned with Liverpool to his former club and bagged four goals in a 6-0 romp on September 28, 1968. The Stourport-born no 9 scored four goals in 22 appearances while at Molineux and had more success after his £100,000 move north during this month. Alan Boswell is the despairing keeper as Les Wilson, Dave Woodfield, sub Bobby Thomson and Derek Parkin also register their agony. Picture courtesy of Liverpool Post and Echo.

Bill McGarry had been Wolves manager for only two months when he tempted Hugh Curran to follow him from East Anglia to Molineux. The Scottish striker signed for £60,000 from Norwich at the end of January, 1969, all of his first four games for the club ending in draws. He had previously played for Millwall and served as an apprentice at Manchester United. Secretary Phil Shaw and ex-Ipswich boss McGarry witness the signing of the forms.

Wolves visited muddy White Hart Lane twice in a month in the late winter of 1968-69, following up a 2-1 FA Cup fourth-round defeat on January 25 with a 1-1 League draw on February 22. The games brought the Knowles brothers, Peter of Wolves and Cyril of Tottenham Hotspur, into opposition at a time when Wanderers were on their way to a final placing of 16th. Derek Parkin is pictured in a close tangle with Alan Gilzean as Bobby Thomson peers between the two.

A week after a Mike O'Grady-secured home win over Albion, Wolves took a point from a creditable goalless draw at Anfield on November 8, 1969, although they had to survive this Tommy Smith free-kick to achieve it. Hugh Curran, Mike Bailey, Paul Walker, Jim McCalliog and a dishevelled Bernard Shaw form the wall, behind which Ian St John is cowering for safety. Picture courtesy of Liverpool Post and Echo.

Bobby Gould marks his first debut for Wolves by leading with his right in the 3-2 defeat at Newcastle on the opening day of the 1970-71 campaign. Defender Ron Guthrie and keeper Iam McFaul are the home duo on a day when Danny Hegan - signed from Albion that summer - was another Wanderers new boy. Gould returned for a second Molineux spell in the mid-1970s. Picture courtesy of Newcastle Chronicle.

The same - but different! It's Derby v Wolves twice at a packed Baseball Ground in January, 1971. Above: Ex-Molineux striker Frank Wignall heads well wide as Frank Munro stands back and lets him get on with it during a 2-1 First Division win secured for Wolves by goals from right-back Bernard Shaw and striker Bobby Gould. John McAlle, John O'Hare, Jim McCalliog and Mike Bailey are also in view. Players from both sides are wearing black armbands after the Ibrox Park disaster that claimed 66 lives a week earlier. Below: A fortnight later, on the 23rd of the month, an FA Cup fifth-round place is at stake as McAlle gratefully boots clear watched by Shaw, Phil Parkes, O'Hare and Munro. The Rams took their revenge in this second meeting with a 2-1 victory. Pictures courtesy of Derby Evening Telegraph.

A colossal leap from Derek Dougan takes him well above the grounded Mike England in Wolves' 2-2 draw with Tottenham on the opening day of the 1971-72 season. The duo also frequently did battle on the international stage with Northern Ireland and Wales respectively. Their clubs were to meet in the UEFA Cup final at the end of a season in which The Doog led the club's goal charts with 24, nine of them in Europe - as many as any player had managed at that time in a European campaign.

BOUNCING BACK

A game with a difference as the long-serving Phil Parkes seems to be having trouble with Mick Jones during Wolves' 0-0 First Division away draw with Leeds on August 21, 1971. Bernard Shaw is the covering defender. And the difference? The game was played at Huddersfield's appropriately-named Leeds Road ground after crowd trouble at Elland Road at a costly defeat at home to Albion at the end of the previous campaign.

Some observers believe George Best rarely found his top form against Wolves, although he got on the score-sheet in this early-season 1-1 Molineux draw in 1971-72. So did the man marking him, Bernard Shaw - the second of only two goals the full-back managed in 156 first-team appearances for the club. This game, watched by 46,471, came four days after Wolves had beaten Manchester City 2-1 at home.

Derek Parkin blasts Wolves 3-1 ahead from the penalty spot in their League Cup second-round tie at Manchester City on September 8, 1971. It was one of only ten goals the full-back notched in his club-record 609 first-team appearances and came on a night when fellow defender John McAlle scored one of his three goals in 508 senior outings. Danny Hegan also got on the score-sheet at Maine Road but Wolves lost 4-3 to the side they were to beat in the 1974 final of the competition.

John Richards flashes in a beauty to help Wolves to a thrilling 2-1 victory over Brian Clough's Derby on November 13 of the Rams' 1971-72 championship-winning season. JR scored both goals in what was the season he notched a total of 16 to announce his arrival on the big stage. The helpless opponents pictured are (from left) Terry Hennessy, John O'Hare, Colin Boulton, John Robson and a grounded Roy McFarland.

No way through for the fearsome Malcolm MacDonald in this sortie towards Phil Parkes's goal in Newcastle's game at Molineux on New Year's Day, 1972. The striker, pursued by Derek Parkin, seems to be miskicking in a game won 2-0 by Bill McGarry's side with goals by Parkin himself and John Richards. It was the third of four successive Wolves wins in a season in which they finished a healthy ninth.

Bernard Shaw finds Phil Parkes with a back-pass in Wolves' famous UEFA Cup triumph over Italian giants Juventus on March 22, 1972. Bill McGarry's side played brilliantly to draw 1-1 in Turin with a Jim McCalliog equaliser and secured quarter-final glory by winning the second leg 2-1 in front of 40,421 enthralled spectators via a Danny Hegan chip and a Derek Dougan header. Juventus, represented in this picture by striker Viola, scored at Molineux through a penalty by Helmut Haller, the inside-forward who had played for West Germany in the 1966 World Cup final and who was reportedly fined £660 after the game at Wolves for late-night drinking.

Lively scenes from Wolves' epic 2-1 victory at home to Leeds in front of a massive 53,379 crowd on Monday, May 8, 1972. Don Revie's mean-machine arrived at Molineux aiming to complete the double after beating Arsenal in the FA Cup final two days before. But they found themselves two down to goals by Frank Munro and Derek Dougan before Billy Bremner got one back. Liverpool drew at Arsenal the same night and Derby - already on holiday in Majorca - were champions. Bremner is seen in discussion with Jim McCalliog and Dave Wagstaffe as Allan Clarke receives treatment.

A largely forgotten game, with a floral backdrop behind the goal! It's Bristol Rovers v Wolves in the Watney Cup pre-season tournament at the long-neglected Eastville Stadium on July 29, 1972. Frank Munro opts for a few seconds' breather in the warm sun as Rovers substitute Bruce Bannister sends Phil Parkes the wrong way with a penalty and secures the Third Division club's 2-0 win. Wolves thrashed the same opposition 4-0 at Molineux in the League Cup three months later.

John McAlle heads away from Tommy Gibb with Phil Parkes covering in this sunny scene as Wolves kick off a League season at Newcastle for the second time in three years. This 1972-73 clash was marked by a goal-scoring debut for Wolves' new boy Steve Kindon but was won 2-1 by the home side. Derek Parkin and John Tudor wait for any crumbs. Picture courtesy of the Newcastle Chronicle/Journal.

John Richards holds off a challenge from Bobby Charlton to power a shot at the Stretford End goal during Wolves' 2-1 First Division defeat at Old Trafford on February 10, 1973. Bernard Shaw and goalscorer Danny Hegan are the gold-shirted men in the background as Manchester United - relegated a season later - gain some revenge for their 2-0 defeat at Molineux in the League in the September and their 1-0 exit there from the FA Cup four months later.

Chelsea's John Phillips was befriended by a black labrador that wandered on to the pitch in this game at Stamford Bridge on March 6, 1973. And the keeper was left feeling as sick as a dog as Derek Dougan wheels away in triumph after scoring one of the goals by which Wolves won 2-0. Jim McCalliog rushes to congratulate the scorer while there are quizzical looks from no 2 Gary Locke, John Hollins, Phillips and Peter Osgood among the ranks of the 1972 FA Cup winners.

Ouch! Jack Charlton was never such a handful as this! It's a time for monkey business at Dudley Zoo as Derek Dougan meets his match in Monty the chimp who, bedecked in Wolves colours, makes a grab for the striker's moustache. The visit came during April, 1973, as Bill McGarry's side homed in on a top-flight final placing of fifth to follow on from their fourth and ninth positions of the previous two seasons.

It's agony as well for Phil Parkes - and Wolves. The veteran keeper, who piled up 382 senior matches during 16 years at Molineux, is attended by coach Sammy Chung and full-backs Derek Parkin and Gerry Taylor during the club's unfortunate FA Cup semi-final defeat against Leeds at Maine Road on April 7, 1973. Billy Bremner scored the only goal for a side who were shock losers in the final against Second Division Sunderland, John Richards later hitting the post.

BOUNCING BACK

Who said football wasn't a dirty game? And this was an Easter Monday fixture, not one in mid-winter! Mike Bailey finds himself covered from head to toe as Wolves become mudlarks to defeat Norwich 3-0 on April 23, 1973. Bill McGarry's side were destined to finish fifth in the First Division and had a young Alan Sunderland on the mark twice two days after they had lost 2-1 at the other East Anglian club, Ipswich. The following day, they played again and lost 2-0 at Stoke.

Images of a long forgotten fixture as Derek Dougan drives past Arsenal keeper Bob Wilson in one of the last stagings of the game to resolve third and fourth places in the FA Cup. This match between the two beaten semi-finalists from 1972-73 was played at Highbury just before the start of the following season and was won 3-1 by Wolves. Dougan scored twice and Jim McCalliog once while Geoff Palmer made his senior debut. Jeff Blockley is the chasing Gunners defender.

It wasn't only against Bournemouth in a famous FA Cup giant-killing tie in 1957 that the Molineux woodwork collapsed. It happened again when Norwich keeper Kevin Keelan collided with his post while unsuccessfully trying to save a 61st minute Derek Dougan lob on the first day of the 1973-74 season. There was a 16-minute delay for rebuilding during which the North Bank choir were in full voice (above) and the unlucky Keelan received treatment. No 3 Derek Parkin, no 7 Jim McCalliog and no 6 John McAlle are the other Wolves players pictured.

Bill McGarry has his "That's another fine mess you've got us into" look in the photo on the right as he and Norwich's Trevor Hockey inspect the damage. Or maybe the manager is doing his impression of a man struck by falling woodwork! Order was eventually restored, with a little help from the police, and all turned out well for Wolves. They went on to win 3-1, with Dougan scoring twice and McCalliog once. Pictures courtesy of Norwich Evening News.

John Richards is quickly on hand to congratulate Derek Dougan on putting Wolves one up on their visit to Southampton on September 1, 1973. The Doog scored five times in the first four games of the season but he was end to the campaign with only ten League goals as his fortunes tailed off. Steve Middleton is the Saints keeper and substitute Steve Kindon the Wolves player in the distance on a day the home side hit back to win 2-1.

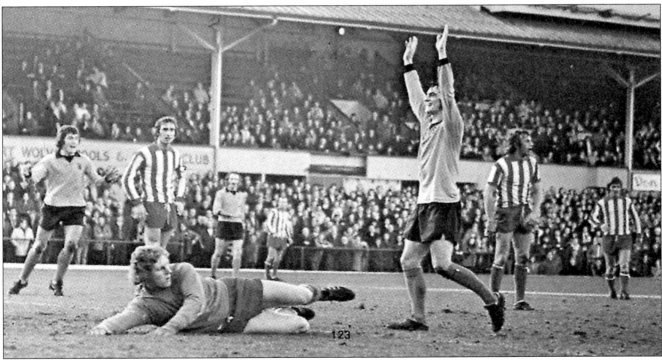

Molineux attracted its then lowest post-war attendance when only 7,623 filed in for this League Cup fourth-round clash with Exeter on November 20, 1973. The game was played on a Tuesday afternoon because of the power shortages caused by a coalminers' strike and brought Wolves what was then their biggest victory in the competition. Kenny Hibbitt is pictured celebrating one of his two goals, the also-pictured John Richards and Derek Dougan netting twice and once respectively.

Dave Wagstaffe's cross is chested down and cracked home by John Richards as Wolves overcome Chelsea 2-0 at Molineux three days before Christmas, 1973. The striker later added a second in a victory that came early in an eight-match unbeaten run in the First Division. Ron Harris and Gary Locke are the visiting defenders unable to close off the route to goal, with Barry Powell lending support to a player with whom he used to share digs in Wolverhampton.

Fearless Frank

LITTLE did Frank Munro know when he scored a hat-trick AGAINST Wolves that he would end up playing 371 competitive games FOR them.

But that's just what happened in the football life of the popular Scot, who also won nine full international caps to go with all his age-group honours north of the border.

He came to the attention of those at Molineux by scoring three times in the final of the Los Angeles Tournament for Aberdeen in 1967. Wolves rattled in six themselves that day to emerge triumphant but had seen enough from a certain strapping six-footer in the opposition ranks to splash out on him the following winter.

Munro approached cult-hero status at Molineux, giving eight years of tremendous service and endorsing the judgement of the man who bought him, Ronnie Allen.

He helped the club reach the UEFA Cup final in 1971-72 and lift the League Cup two years later, going on to play 33 games in the 1976-77 Second Division title-winning campaign.

No wonder Wolverhampton Wanderers supporters remember Fearless Frank Munro with such affection.

Frank Munro threatens keeper Eric McManus (above) during Wolves' 3-0 friendly win at Notts County on August 5, 1972. To the left is Peter Eastoe. Wolves had experienced a hectic close season, playing four exhibition matches in North America in May and then going to New Zealand and Australia the following month for more games.

Even the eyes of the law are on Munro (left) as he is watched all the way to the tunnel after being sent off in the 1-1 draw at home to Stoke on February 2, 1974. Fortunately, the Scot, dismissed for a 60th minute off-the-ball offence, won an appeal against being suspended for the League Cup final a few weeks later - much to the relief of centre-half partner John McAlle, who is to be seen in the white coat on the front row of the upper tier of the old Waterloo Road Stand.

One proud Scotsman. Frank Munro added nine full international caps to the 371 competitive games he played for Wolves and cuts an impressive figure here as he strides out for a Home International clash with England at Wembley on May 24, 1975. The game was won 5-1 by the home side, the popular centre-half returning to the Molineux line-up at home to a newly-promoted Manchester United on the opening day of the following season.

Frank Munro's face breaks into a grin as Wolves take the lead over their then big rivals Coventry in the penultimate home game of 1973-74. The ball was despatched past Sky Blues keeper Bill Glazier by the stooping David Cross for an own goal that delighted the arms-raised Steve Kindon. The game was drawn 1-1 but was followed three days later by a Molineux victory over another Midlands side, Leicester, as Bill McGarry's men finished a satisfactory 12th.

Wolves were still looking for their first victory of 1975-76 when they drew 0-0 with Arsenal on August 30 in front of only 18,144. Gunners keeper Jimmy Rimmer is thankful to hold on in this attack as Frank Munro, watched by Steve Kindon and John Richards, takes a tumble. Arsenal's no 6 is David O'Leary, recently better known as a manager. Wolves had to wait another fortnight before their eighth game of the campaign brought them their opening win.

League Cup Glory 1974

IN FOUR seasons from August, 1970, Wolves played a staggering 58 cup-ties - the most memorable of them by far their Wembley showdown against Manchester City on March 2, 1974.

Having won the Texaco Cup in 1970-71, reached the UEFA Cup final in 1971-72 and gone out in the semi-final of both the FA Cup and League Cup in 1972-73, Wolves breathed a sigh of relief when the big breakthrough finally came.

They had not won a major competition since the 1959-60 FA Cup but Bill McGarry's team put that right by lifting the League Cup 14 years on.

As befitting the happy Wanderers at the time, there were plenty of goals, with John Richards's seven, including his winner at the Twin Towers, leading the way in the victorious campaign. It was a standard even a Manchester City side boasting Denis Law, Rodney Marsh and Francis Lee couldn't match!

The real hero of Wembley, 1974, was Gary Pierce, who celebrated his 23rd birthday on the same day with an outstanding performance against star-studded Manchester City. His was a display that Bill McGarry recognised at the end by running on to the pitch and hugging him! Here, Pierce dives on a cross, watched by John McAlle and City forward Denis Law.

LEAGUE CUP GLORY 1974

High-kicking antics from Derek Parkin, Mike Summerbee and Wolves skipper Mike Bailey during the 1974 League Cup final triumph on March 2, 1974. John McAlle waits to join the action on the right. Kenny Hibbitt's volley opened the scoring in the first half, Colin Bell drove in the equaliser and John Richards took careful aim to rifle home a late winner.

Wolves chairman John Ireland, later to have a stand named after him at Molineux, indulges in the ultimate celebration as he sips champagne from the League Cup during the festivities that followed the victory over Manchester City. Looking on are Barbara and Mike Bailey. Richards didn't play again that season because of injury but ended it with 18 goals, seven of them in the League Cup.

Testing Times

A sitter with a difference! John Richards makes himself comfortable as he touches in the only goal of the game on Wolves' League visit to Chelsea on September 28, 1974. It was the club's first win in nine games in all competitions, during which time they had lost their grip on the League Cup - beaten at home by Fulham. Keeper John Phillips, Ron Harris and John Dempsey are the horrified defenders.

Get in! It's not the prettiest goal Steve Kindon ever saw and celebrated as a Wolves player but he is not complaining as Frank Munro forces the ball over the line despite the efforts of Peter Shilton and John Marsh in the 2-2 First Division draw at the Victoria Ground on February 15, 1975. Also in close attendance for Stoke are Mike Pejic and Ian Moores on an afternoon when Kenny Hibbitt scored Wolves' other goal.

TESTING TIMES

Phil Parkes flies across his area and keeps his goal intact at QPR on April 5, 1975. But it's not the Wolves version! Gary Pierce was between the posts for the visitors at Loftus Road, where Rangers' Sedgley-born ex-Walsall man - capped once by England and later to serve West Ham - helped deny the leaping Frank Munro. Peter Withe and Steve Daley are the other Wolves players. Rangers won 2-0.

John McAlle lets out a yell of despair as Francis Lee bundles in the only goal of Wolves' clash at Derby on April 9, 1975. Derek Parkin, Geoff Palmer and Gary Pierce are the trio on the line unable to help. The Rams also won 1-0 at Molineux in the January and went on to win the championship for the second time in four seasons. Picture courtesy of Derby Evening Telegraph.

Wolves had become poor travellers by the time they visited Carlisle for their final away game of 1974-75. This 1-0 loss - the last of Peter Withe's 17 games for the club - was the sixth successive trip on which they had been beaten. From left, Willie Carr, Mike Bailey, a distant Steve Kindon and Kenny Hibbitt watch Derek Jefferson preparing to put in his challenge. The Cumbrians were relegated that spring after only one year in the top flight. Picture courtesy of Carlisle Evening News.

An emotional farewell for the darling of the North Bank....Derek Dougan wreaks havoc for the final time as a Wolves player as he is given a sentimental run-out as substitute in the last of his 323 senior outings of the club. He had his sights on a 124th Wanderers goal with this shot in the 1-1 draw at home to Leeds on April 26, 1975, but it was John Richards, pictured in the background between The Doog and Paul Madeley, who netted for Wolves. It was a slow wind-down for Dougan, who made only three League starts that season.

How high was that! Ian Ross, later to join the Molineux backroom team, complains at the raising of Norman Bell's boot after veteran Aston Villa left-back Charlie Aitken had been caught and left needing treatment in the goalless First Division draw on September 23, 1975. Frank Carrodus faces the camera while, in the background to the right of Bell, is Brian Little - caretaker Wolves manager in 1986. Bill McGarry's side had beaten Birmingham 2-0 at home ten days earlier.

Vintage Kenny Hibbitt! Everton keeper Dai Davies takes off to his right but can't stop this fizzer from Wolves' long-serving midfielder flying into his net on October 25, 1975. Unfortunately for Bill McGarry's side, the Hibbitt special wasn't enough to stave off a 2-1 home defeat that kept the team struggling near the foot of the table after they had won only two of their opening 14 League games of the campaign.

Wolves may have struggled in the First Division in 1975-76 but they had a good FA Cup run and savoured this 3-0 third-round triumph at home to Arsenal. Here's goal no 2, delivered from the feared right boot of John Richards, who just beats Pat Rice's attempt at a last-ditch block after leaving David O'Leary grounded. Norman Bell, who was also on target, is the team-mate in closest support of the scorer.

Okay, it's wide! Phil Parkes watches Ipswich striker Trevor Whymark run out of pitch in the FA Cup fourth-round clash at Portman Road on January 24, 1976. Alan Sunderland, unusually, is the right-back doing the jockeying and John McAlle, Derek Parkin and Mike Bailey are the other gold-shirted players on hand. In the far background is George Burley. Wolves drew 0-0 but lost 3-0 in Suffolk in the League less than a month later. Picture courtesy of Ipswich Evening Star.

TESTING TIMES

A fluke, but Wolves weren't complaining....even John Richards looks surprised as Bobby Gould's cross deceives West Midlands-born keeper Paul Cooper and drops into the net for the only goal of Wolves' FA Cup fourth-round replay against Ipswich on January 27, 1976. John Wark (left) and Mick Mills are the helpless defenders in what proved to be Mike Bailey's last FA Cup tie for the club. The East Anglians had won 2-1 at Molineux in the previous season's competition.

A Molineux winner for Norman Bell in the Staffordshire derby against Stoke on the last day of January, 1976. The striker scored 24 goals in exactly 100 senior appearances for the club from 1975 to 1982, this one floating over Peter Shilton on a day when Willie Carr also netted and Gerry O'Hara played the first of his nine League matches for the club. The Stoke no 5 just to the right of Bell is Alan Dodd, who was later to become a popular figure at Wolves.

Wolves have enjoyed an excellent record against Burnley over the years and, in their hour of need, they beat them 3-2 at Molineux on February 21, 1976. Norman Bell nets this goal to go with a brace from John Richards, the Lancashire side finding themselves on the receiving end of a double after being thrashed 5-1 in the Turf Moor mud back in mid-November. Sadly, the two clubs were to be relegated together, Wolves finishing 20th.

A massive 59,433 crowd were present at Old Trafford as Manchester United and Wolves did battle in the sixth round of the FA Cup on March 6, 1976. Stewart Houston climbs above Steve Kindon and United keeper Alex Stepney in this Wolves attack, watched by the grounded Brian Greenhoff (left) and Gordon Hill. John Richards opened the scoring and Phil Parkes was inspired as he kept out everything thrown at him until a deflected late equaliser by Gerry Daly.

The Molineux atmosphere was electric for the Wolves v United replay and the signs were good when Steve Kindon lunged in front of Brian Greenhoff and Martin Buchan to head the home side into the lead. The also-pictured John Richards made it 2-0 and Kindon later rattled the woodwork but United regained their composure and hit back to win 3-2 en route for a shock odd-goal defeat in the final against Southampton. This was the third time Wolves had led United 2-0 in an FA Cup tie at Molineux and still lost.

Four days after FA Cup elimination, relegation-threatened Wolves travelled to Sheffield United and gave their survival hopes a shot in the arm with a 4-1 win, completed by this late floating header by Steve Kindon. Colin Franks challenges, with Alan Woodward and Jim Brown as the other helpless United players on a day when Kindon, full-back Geoff Palmer and John Richards scored the other goals. It was all to no avail. Wolves went down, so did the Blades.

Relegation was close when Wolves visited West Ham on April 3, 1976, and ground out a dull 0-0 draw. One month and one day later, it became a mathematical certainty as they famously lost 3-1 at Molineux to a Liverpool side who became champions on the same night. Here, Alan Sunderland climbs above Frank Lampard Snr, with Steve Kindon, Graham Paddon and Trevor Brooking having a close view.

John Richards was certainly not to blame for Wolves' 1975-76 demise. This equaliser that flashed past Arsenal keeper Jimmy Rimmer was his last but one goal of a season that ended with 25 against his name. Wolves lost 2-1 at Highbury in the April 13 clash, followed up by crashing 3-1 at Coventry, beating visiting Norwich 1-0 and then going down to Liverpool in front of 48,918 spectators on the night Birmingham drew at Sheffield United and narrowly survived.

The defiant last stand. John Richards swings his right boot, completes his fourth hat-trick of the six he recorded for the club and rounds off a spectacular 5-0 demolition of Newcastle on April 10, 1976. Kenny Hibbitt and Willie Carr also found the target, but it wasn't enough to prevent the end of Wolves' nine-year stint back in the top flight. Bill McGarry, manager for nearly eight years of that span, resigned after relegation had been confirmed.

Second Division Champions

Welcome to the Second Division! By coincidence, a relegated Wolves side now under the management of Sammy Chung kicked off in the lower grade in August, 1976, against the two clubs who had taken the drop with them. They drew 0-0 at home to Burnley, then shared the points 2-2 at Sheffield United in midweek, when Alan Sunderland scored this beauty - much to the approval of Steve Daley in the background.

Alan Sunderland was again on hand as Wolves netted at Nottingham Forest four days later on August 28, 1976 - but he was just following up here as the hidden Bobby Gould scored one of his two goals in a 3-1 win. John McGovern, skipper during Forest's subsequent glory years under Brian Clough, is seen sliding in too late while the keeper is Peter Wells. Chung backed the relegated side to bounce back at the first go and had made no new signings that summer.

SECOND DIVISION CHAMPIONS

Bobby Gould rises perfectly to beat a defender and find the net on his way to scoring twice in a 3-0 home win over Charlton on September 4, 1976. Wolves quickly found Second Division life comfortable and Gould found made himself at home faster than most. His goal tally was in double figures before Christmas but he was sold to Second Division rivals Bristol Rovers in mid-season, having totalled 39 goals in 93 appearances in his two Molineux stints.

The demolition of Charlton is complete in front of a 15,652 attendance as Alan Sunderland sidefoots into an empty net in the dying minutes to make it two wins and two draws from the opening four League matches. In the meantime, there had been a blip at home to Sheffield Wednesday in the second round of the League Cup - a third successive defeat against opponents from outside the top flight after Wolves had won the competition in 1974.

There were no goals at Fulham for the visit of Wolves on the now poignant date of September 11. But this 1976-77 clash certainly did not lack attacking riches. Sammy Chung's side had scored eight goals in their previous three games and the Londoners had George Best and no 10 Rodney Marsh in their line-up. It was left to John McAlle to lunge in here and keep the former Manchester United idol under control, watched by Kenny Hibbitt. Picture courtesy of Ken Coton.

Jovial Gary Pierce is joined by a cuddly companion as he strides out to take his place in front of the North Bank for the home game against Oldham on September 18, 1976. 'Henry' was given to the keeper by two female fans and certainly proved a lucky mascot, Pierce playing all 48 of the club's League and cup games in this promotion season. It was slaughter in the sun for Oldham, who were despatched 5-0 as Steve Kindon led the way with two.

A sobering night for Wolves as they are hammered 6-2 by visiting Southampton on October 5, 1976 - only three days after they themselves had won 6-1 in the League away to Hereford. Former Molineux favourite Jim McCalliog (right) is an onlooker as Saints' on-loan Derby keeper Colin Boulton punches clear from Alan Sunderland and no 9 Bobby Gould. Wolves also lost their next game, at Hull, but were soon back on the right trail.

Missile-throwing fans caused referee Johnson to lead Blackpool and Wolves off for eight second-half minutes in their clash at Bloomfield Road on October 30, 1976. Willie Carr and Alan Sunderland wear concerned expressions with their side trailing 2-1. But the bumper illumination-season crowd of 21,005 saw an equaliser on the day goals by Frank Munro and Kenny Hibbitt earned a 2-2 draw. The downside was that this was Mike Bailey's 436th and final Wolves game.

The Molineux promotion bandwagon was well and truly rolling by the time Wolves went to Bristol Rovers' old Eastville home and romped to this 5-1 December 27 win. Steve Kindon can't believe it as his 50-yard run comes to an end with a near miss but he scored along with Alan Sunderland (2), Kenny Hibbitt and Steve Daley. In their previous two away games, cavalier Wolves had won 4-2 at Orient and drawn 3-3 at Chelsea.

SECOND DIVISION CHAMPIONS

The combination of Kenny Hibbitt's leg and Gary Pierce's brave punch clear Wolves' lines during their 1-1 draw at Millwall on New Year's Day, 1977. Hibbitt was his side's scorer at The Den - one of an incredible 18 goals he netted that season. From a prolific midfield, Steve Daley contributed 14 and Alan Sunderland, who played up front on occasions, 16. Sunderland and an on-the-line Geoff Palmer are the other Wolves players pictured.

The last competitive Molineux sighting of George Best came in this 5-1 home victory over Fulham on February 19, 1977. It was Wolves' sixth success of the season by four goals or more and summed up the goal power in the side at the time, Steve Daley and Kenny Hibbitt scoring twice and John Richards once. Willie Carr is the man challenging Best in the late-winter mud. Picture courtesy of Ken Coton.

Wolves didn't just excel in the promotion race in 1976-77 - they also made good progress in the FA Cup. After knocking out Rotherham and Ipswich at Molineux, they sent Third Division Chester packing 1-0 via another Kenny Hibbitt goal. Geoff Palmer is pictured on a right-wing gallop in a victory which was followed by a sixth-round clash with visiting Leeds and a narrow defeat. The Chester game ended John Richards' run of scoring in six successive FA Cup ties.

One for the record books.....youngster Ken Todd nets the only goal of his five-game Wolves first-team career. This conversion of a Kenny Hibbitt pull-back comes in a 2-1 Molineux victory over Hereford in the latter stages of Wolves' Second Division promotion triumph on March 12, 1977. Hibbitt scored the other goal as Wolves embarked on another run of seven League matches unbeaten after losing at Luton the previous week. That was their first defeat in 17 games in all competitions.

SECOND DIVISION CHAMPIONS

Alan Sunderland uses his good balance to twist a way between Leeds duo Frank Gray (left) and Paul Reaney in the FA Cup sixth-round tie at Molineux on March 19, 1977. Sammy Chung's side were on a run of four successive League victories at the time but found their old rivals too hot to handle and were beaten by the only goal of the game in front of a crowd of 49,770.

Job done! Manager Sammy Chung and chairman Harry Marshall crack open the champagne and kick-start the celebrations in the visitors' dressing-room at Home Park after Wolves had clinched promotion with their goalless draw with Plymouth on April 30, 1977. Three games of the League season remained at the time, the first of them bringing a 1-0 defeat at Southampton in the second leg of the southern 'tour' three days later.

Left: A sad end to Wolves keeper Gary Pierce's ever-present 1976-77 season as he is carried off late in the champions' last-day 1-0 win at Bolton by physio Kevin Walters and coach Brian Owen. An early Kenny Hibbitt goal at packed Burnden Park delighted the 8,000 travelling fans but hit Bolton hard. They stayed down while Nottingham Forest went up.

Below: A partially recovered Pierce shows off the Second Division winners' trophy at Wolves' centenary celebration clash with Manchester City on May 23. Phil Parkes was back in goal for the start of 1977-78 and Pierce played only three more times for Wolves, all in 1978-79.

Back in the Big Time

"WE KNEW we were good enough to come straight back up, so we didn't chase any new signings." So says Sammy Chung when looking back at the triumphant return to top-flight football he oversaw at Molineux in 1976-77.

As a far cry from today's necessity of having to reach for the cheque-book to cope with the onslaught of Premiership stars and then shedding big-name players if relegation comes to pass, Wolves opted for stability a quarter of a century ago.

The long-serving Bill McGarry paid for the club's 1976 demotion with his job but little else changed. Wolves were happy to run with what they had when they went down and there were no major additions after they had won the Second Division title under McGarry's popular long-time no 2.

"I remember telling the directors that I thought we had enough to get us back up," Chung recalls today. He was seen to be a good judge as his players blazed a thrilling goal-laden path and made short work of a grade of competition they hadn't seen for nearly a decade.

Even when they regained their place among the elite at a time when Liverpool, rather than Manchester United and Arsenal, were ruling the championship roost, purchases were scarce. Keeper Paul Bradshaw came in during the autumn and striker Bill Rafferty followed in the winter. Otherwise, the job of consolidation was left to the tried-and-trusted names.

It was a task that was accomplished with a respectable final placing of 15th place, although there were some anxious weeks before Chung's men won their last three League games to banish any lingering fears of relegation.

Wolves were back where their supporters believed they belonged and were to enjoy some golden times in the next four seasons before the next big dip in their fortunes.

A joyous moment for John Richards as he climbs above Billy Bonds to head the 100th League goal of his Wolves career. This effort came in a 2-2 draw at home to West Ham on October 15, 1977, and is closely watched by Tommy Taylor and Norman Bell. Sammy Chung's side were in an up-and-down phase at the time but Richards was in a prolific run, netting a hat-trick against Leicester just before and a brace at Manchester City in the next game after the visit of the Hammers.

Wolves won their first two games of 1977-78 and remained in mid-table towards the end of autumn, but suffered three consecutive defeats from the start of December, culminating in this 4-0 thrashing at Newcastle in their last game before Christmas. Irving Nattrass outjumps John McAlle to start the St James's Park rot, watched by Steve Daley and Mel Eves. Picture courtesy of Newcastle Chronicle and Journal.

A cry of anguish from Steve Daley as he is pipped to the ball in the Exeter area during Wolves' FA Cup third-round tie at St James's Park in January, 1978. On an awkward afternoon in Devon, Wolves did have a Daly on target - Maurice Daly - as he and Willie Carr scored the goals that took the Third Division club back to Molineux for a replay.

Memorable moment for Bob Hazell as he climbs above England centre-half Dave Watson to head the only goal of his 37-game Wolves first-team career. This effort came in a 1-1 draw at home to Manchester City on March 18, 1978, four days after a Molineux draw with Albion by the same score. But Wolves then slipped into relegation danger as they lost five matches in a row and climbed back to 15th only after a winning end to their programme.

It looks like yet another John Richards goal but Mel Eves struck this late and vital equaliser at Stamford Bridge in Wolves' 1-1 draw against Chelsea on April 22, 1978. Sammy Chung's men were fighting for top-flight survival at the time, so no wonder (from left) Martin Patching and Billy Rafferty were all eyes as the ball flew goalwards. Micky Droy is unable to cut it out while Peter Bonetti - later to become a goalkeeper coach at Molineux - and Ray Wilkins (right) are also in the picture.

John Richards is congratulated by fellow marksman Mel Eves after scoring against Aston Villa in the final home League game of 1977-78. Keeper Jimmy Rimmer and midfielder Gordon Cowans - the latter to serve Wolves more than 16 years later - are bystanders as Richards celebrates his first League goal since the Boxing Day victory at home to Leeds. He finished with a relatively modest 13 goals but was still the club's top scorer as they used this derby to ensure top-flight survival.

Wolves come under pressure at sunny Southampton in their problem-filled start to 1978-79. Ted MacDougall dives to send a twisting header against George Berry as John McAlle, Phil Boyer, Peter Daniel and Norman Bell look on. Daniel and Bell scored but this 3-2 Dell defeat was one of six losses the side suffered in their first seven League matches. There was also a first-hurdle League Cup exit at Fourth Division Reading. Picture courtesy of Southern Evening Echo.

Steve Daley lunges in bravely in a battlefield of a Manchester United goalmouth but Jimmy Nicholl repels this moment of danger with a hefty clearance in the League clash at Molineux on October 28, 1978. Daley notched his first goal of the season in this game and Kenny Hibbitt (background) was also on target but United emerged victorious and won 4-2 in keeper Gary Pierce's final Wanderers appearance.

Football was savaged by the weather in the early weeks of 1979 as Britain shivered in its worst winter since 1963. But Wolves had the go-ahead to face Everton in this League game in the snow on February 3 and Steve Daley kept a sure footing to hit the only goal. Kenny Hibbitt maintains his balance here to shake off Bob Latchford as George Berry looks on. John Barnwell had replaced Sammy Chung three months earlier.

John Richards, who slammed a right-foot Wembley winner against Manchester City five years earlier, tries for a repeat against the same opponents in a League game at Maine Road on another tricky pitch showing the effects of the harsh 1978-79 elements. But the covering Tommy Booth charged this shot down and City won 3-1 despite a goal for the visitors from Kenny Hibbitt. This game came a week and a half after the clubs had drawn 1-1 at Molineux.

It was West Midlands might v Shropshire's finest when Wolves and Shrewsbury squared up for an FA Cup quarter-final collision in March, 1979. A gate of 40,946 made sure it was a bumper pay-day for the visitors, who were managed and skippered by Graham Turner. The man who was to be boss at Molineux from 1986 to 1994 had his eyes on goal with this powerful right-foot shot that was blocked in a worried goalmouth (above) populated by John McAlle, Paul Bradshaw, Geoff Palmer and George Berry. And it's Turner again (below) as he climbs above Berry to power a header towards the target. The game was drawn 1-1, Bill Rafferty scoring for Wolves and Ian Atkins converting a penalty for a club who were to win promotion that season and so reach the giddy heights of the old Second Division.

There was no mistake by Wolves second time round as they romped to a 3-1 win at the Gay Meadow in the replay on March 13. Rafferty netted again, along with Peter Daniel and Willie Carr, and Shrewsbury's consolation came too late to matter. Here, McAlle bravely blocks an Atkins shot, with Kenny Hibbitt, Daniel and Rafferty around him. Graham Turner is on the far right. Wolves had earlier beaten Brighton, Newcastle and Crystal Palace in their Cup run.

John Richards rises unchallenged to head home and extract a useful point from a 1-1 spring-time draw with high-riding Albion at The Hawthorns. The striker, flanked by Steve Daley, missed almost all the first half of the season through injury but his nine goals from then on helped keep the club up. Alistair Robertson, later to captain Wolves, and John Wile are the Baggies defenders.

Three Wolves stalwarts are caught in the frame during Wolves' unhappy 2-0 FA Cup semi-final eclipse by Arsenal at Villa Park on March 31, 1979. Alan Sunderland, who scored one of the Gunners' second-half goals, finds Derek Parkin competing shoulder to shoulder with him as John McAlle keeps an eye on proceedings. Between them, the trio amassed 1,315 first-team appearances for the club and there was to be Wembley glory for Sunderland, the junior partner, when he scored the winner in a memorable final against Manchester United.

Sam Allardyce and the sliding Tony Dunne - the latter a veteran of Manchester United's 1968 European Cup winning team against Benfica at Wembley - are powerless to prevent John Richards driving Wolves' goal past keeper Jim McDonagh in the 1-1 draw at home to Bolton on April 28, 1979. The point came as Wolves limped to a final placing of 18th in a season of managerial change. Kenny Hibbitt and Billy Rafferty are also pictured.

A famous new face appeared in Wolves colours for 1979-80 - Emlyn Hughes. The Liverpool and England star wore no 5 on his debut for the trip to Derby, which resulted in a 1-0 win thanks to Wayne Clarke's goal. Steve Carter and Aidan McCaffery are the Rams duo trying to force a way past Hughes and George Berry. This was a delayed first game of the season, Wolves being prevented from facing Ipswich at home on the scheduled kick-off day by building work on the John Ireland Stand. Picture courtesy of Derby Evening Telegraph.

After Ipswich had been despatched 3-0 at Molineux, Wolves suffered their first defeat of 1979-80 when Bristol City beat them 2-0 at Ashton Gate on September 1. It proved to be a relegation campaign for the West Countrymen, who have Joe Royle surrounded by Wayne Clarke, George Berry, Willie Carr and Martin Patching in this picture. Wolves bounced back by winning 3-2 at both Everton and Arsenal in their next two away games.

Mel Eves leaps high off the ground in celebration of Kenny Hibbitt's equaliser against Manchester United on September 22, 1979. Andy Gray and John Richards scored further goals and ensured an impressive 3-1 victory. Gary Bailey is the hapless keeper for the beaten 1979 FA Cup finalists, Wolves at the time also taking the first couple of steps in their famous League Cup-winning run under John Barnwell and Richie Barker.

Nottingham Forest v Wolves in 1979-80 - but not THAT meeting! This was a League clash on October 6 at the City Ground, where the visitors continued their prolific early-season scoring form with goals from Peter Daniel and John Richards. Unfortunately, Brian Clough's team of European Cup holders netted three. Here, George Berry and Mel Eves patrol as Paul Bradshaw dives on a cross to deny Scottish international Kenny Burns. Picture courtesy of Nottingham Evening Post.

Wolves had to head back for Derby's Baseball Ground on the night of December 18, 1979, this time for a League Cup quarter-final second replay with Grimsby. It was a match that pulled in a 16,475 crowd, the clubs having drawn at both Blundell Park and Molineux. Then, goals from John Richards - seen here holding off Dean Crombie - and Kenny Hibbitt saw Wolves make safe progess at the neutral venue. The Humbersiders were in Division Three at the time.

One of the big moments from Wolves' 3-1 FA Cup third-round victory at Division Two Notts County on January 5, 1980. Colin Brazier takes avoiding action and Trevor Christie and Magpies no 7 Iain McCulloch have no chance to intervene as George Berry crashes in one of only six goals he scored during his Wanderers career. This shot made it 1-0, John Richards and Willie Carr rounding off the scoring.

Vital moment for Wolves in their League Cup semi-final first leg at Swindon on January 22, 1980, as Andy Gray celebrates the equaliser just scored by the also-pictured Peter Daniel. The Third Division side - shock winners of the competition at Arsenal's expense 11 years earlier - had taken the lead and were to do so for a second time as they won 2-1 in front of 25,786 spectators at the County Ground.

Wolves were the scourge of Norfolk in the winter of 1979-80, preceding a 4-0 League crushing of Norwich with this 3-2 FA Cup fourth-round replay win on January 30. There are tense looks at the wrong end here as Justin Fashanu hooks in a shot under pressure from Derek Parkin, Emlyn Hughes and keeper Paul Bradshaw. George Berry, one of the visitors' scorers, covers the line while England World Cup hero Martin Peters hovers. Picture courtesy of Norwich Evening News.

Wembley is firmly within Wolves' sights as John Richards tucks the second of his two goals past Swindon keeper Jimmy Allan in a tense League Cup semi-final second leg in front of 41,031 at Molineux on February 12, 1980. This was the last but one of Richards' club record 18 goals in the competition. Mel Eves had earlier opened the scoring on a night when a 3-1 victory spelled a 4-3 aggregate success and sent Wolves to Wembley for the fifth time.

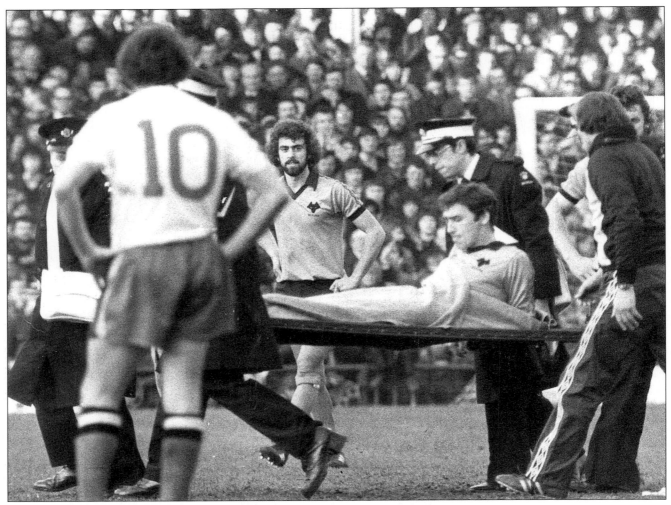

Four days after their memorable triumph in one knockout, Wolves crashed out of another - 3-0 at home to Graham Taylor's Watford in an FA Cup fifth-round tie. Mick Kearns made his debut in goal for Wolves, whose defeat was all the sadder for the departure of sub John McAlle with a broken leg that kept him out until the following January. The injury deprived the Liverpudlian, who is watched here by a sympathetic Geoff Palmer and Peter Daniel, of any chance of a second League Cup final appearance. He played only a further 17 League games for the club and joined Sheffield United for £10,000 in August, 1981.

Wolves defend in depth during their 4-0 League victory over Norwich at Carrow Road on February 23, 1980. Peter Daniel is the man challenging 1966 England World Cup final goalscorer Martin Peters in the air, with (from left) Kevin Reeves, George Berry, Geoff Palmer, Derek Parkin and Emlyn Hughes on hand for the loose ball. John Barnwell's side were inspired on the road and had won two weeks earlier at Manchester United. Picture courtesy of the Norwich Evening News.

Emlyn Hughes, this is your life! Wolves' League Cup-winning captain receives the red-book treatment from Eamonn Andrews as he walks off following a 1-0 home win over his former club Liverpool on February 26, 1980. The 62-cap England defender was whisked to the neighbouring Wolves Social Club for the first-ever This is Your Life to be recorded outside London. Among the guests were Kevin Keegan, Joe Mercer and even Grand National winner Red Rum. Hughes was the third Wolves player after Billy Wright and Ron Flowers to captain England after the Second World War, Bill Slater skippering the country at amateur level.

League Cup Glory 1980

Trevor Francis, who had scored a European Cup final winner the previous spring, gallops across the Wembley turf, hotly pursued by Geoff Palmer, as Nottingham Forest aim to add the 1980 League Cup to their list of honours under Brian Clough. Wolves had other ideas, though, and won 1-0. Forest put the defeat behind them and retained their European crown in Munich a few weeks later.

Below: It's George Berry sliding to the rescue as he seals off a run by Garry Birtles towards Paul Bradshaw's goal. The plan to smother Cloughie's star-studded forwards worked a treat for Wolves, who kept a clean sheet for the fifth time in their victorious campaign. The other gold-shirted players are (from left) John Richards, Kenny Hibbitt and Geoff Palmer. Pictures courtesy of Nottingham Evening Post.

LEAGUE CUP GLORY 1980

The latest score is there for all to see as Martin O'Neill - a highly intelligent player before he became a highly articulate and successful manager - tries his luck with a free-kick that Wolves defend with a four-man wall of (from left) Peter Daniel, Willie Carr, Kenny Hibbitt and Mel Eves. To the left is Derek Parkin. Picture courtesy of Nottingham Evening Post.

Below: Kenny Hibbitt is in appealing mood as Garry Birtles lets fly at the target before George Berry can get across and protect the route to goal. Picture courtesy of Nottingham Evening Post.

Tense moments in Wolves' goalmouth as Nottingham Forest's Ian Bowyer darts between Emlyn Hughes and Paul Bradshaw. The other players pictured are (from left) Martin O'Neill, George Berry and Garry Birtles. Picture courtesy of Nottingham Evening Post.

Heading for a Fall

A fortnight after their Wembley triumph, Wolves saw off another Midlands club when they went to Coventry and won 3-1 in the League. Six-times-capped Scottish international Willie Carr, playing against the club where he made his name, leaves Gary Gillespie trailing, draws keeper Jim Blyth and squares for John Richards (partly hidden) to make it 2-0. Richards scored twice as part of his 18-goal haul for the season and, on the same day, Hugh Atkinson netted the first of his three goals for the club.

Derby joy for Mel Eves as he savours his equaliser with Wolves fans in the League game at Villa on September 20, 1980. At his side stands John Richards while no 12 Wayne Clarke trots back for the restart and Gordon Cowans despairs. John Barnwell's side lost 2-1 but went on to a final 1979-80 placing of sixth. Three nights earlier, Wolves had lost 3-1 in a UEFA Cup first-round tie in Eindhoven.

No luck for no 10 John Richards and no 9 Wayne Clarke as they toil for a breakthrough in the First Division game at Manchester United on November 12, 1980. Arthur Albiston, Kevin Moran, Mick Duxbury, Mickey Thomas and Sammy McIlroy comprise the all-star Old Trafford cast in the photo, taken in a night fixture as Wolves added a useful point to the maximum they had taken when beating United 1-0 in their first home game of the season.

A wonderful night for Emlyn Hughes is highlighted as he aims a close-range shot between his former team-mates Phil Thompson and Ray Clemence for Wolves' final goal in a memorable 4-1 win over reigning Football League champions Liverpool on November 25, 1980. Mel Eves, another of the scorers on the night, looks on as the ex-Anfield hero continues to make a name for himself at his new club.

Stoke slain! Above: Paul Bradshaw lunges towards the ball and the feet of Lee Chapman as Wolves come under threat in their snowbound 1-0 victory over the Potters on November 29, 1980. Emlyn Hughes, a half-hidden Colin Brazier and Peter Daniel are the nearest covering players while Paul Bracewell and Sammy McIlroy are up in support for the visitors. The only goal came from Norman Bell. Below: Mel Eves has a look of grim satisfaction as he hooks the ball past the flying Peter Fox for Wolves' winner in their FA Cup third-round replay against the same opponents in January, 1981. The old Staffordshire rivals had drawn 2-2 three days earlier but this strike, and another from Kenny Hibbitt, settled the issue. Former Manchester City veteran Mike Doyle is the Stoke defender standing to the right as Bell looks on.

The tide is turned as Wolves, having lost three League matches in a row and conceded four in the latest two of them, despatch Middlesbrough 3-0 at Molineux on January 10, 1981. Kenny Hibbitt scored one but the hero of the hour was Mel Eves, who is pictured netting one of his two goals. The Wednesbury-born forward scored 53 times in 214 senior outings for the club, who were recording their first win in six League matches.

A goal and a 2-1 victory for Wolves in their FA Cup revenge mission against Watford on January 27, 1981. Graham Taylor's side had run out handsome winners at Molineux almost 12 months earlier but this fourth-round replay goes the way of John Barnwell's men as an 89th minute drive past Steve Sherwood by Derek Parkin proves to be the winner. Andy Gray jumps for joy, his strike-partner John Richards having scored the other goal after the sides had drawn 1-1 at Vicarage Road.

HEADING FOR A FALL

Having beaten Middlesbrough exactly two months earlier in the League, Wolves defeated them 3-1 in an FA Cup quarter-final replay in March, 1981. John Richards was able to toast the last of his 24 FA Cup goals for the club on a night when Molineux hosted its last 40,000-plus gate. Fellow scorer Norman Bell is ready to extend his congratulations while Andy Gray - on target in the 1-1 draw at Ayresome Park three days earlier - celebrates in the background with the other marksman, Mel Eves.

End of the FA Cup road for Wolves as they are thumped 3-0 in their semi-final replay against Tottenham at 'neutral' Highbury on April 15, 1981. The teams drew 2-2 at Hillsborough but this Garth Crooks header opened the scoring four days later, Spurs going on to beat Manchester City in the 100th FA Cup final. Geoff Palmer, Paul Bradshaw and George Berry are the Wolves trio, with no 5 Ricky Villa, no 7 Ossie Ardiles and no 8 Steve Archibald the other Tottenham men.

Hands on from Hansen. Liverpool's long-time elegant defender and the BBC's long-time eloquent pundit Alan Hansen gets up close to John Richards on Wolves' Division One visit to Anfield on January 16, 1982. Looking on is another Scouse-Scot Graeme Souness, with Paul Bradshaw the keeper in the distance. The Merseysiders won 2-1 and went on to lift their fifth League title in seven years despite Hugh Atkinson's only goal of the season.

A painful landing for Paul Bradshaw as he emerges in some discomfort from a tussle with Coventry striker Steve Whitton in the goalless First Division draw at Highfield Road on March 27, 1982. Andy Gray and Geoff Palmer are on hand as two of the other senior professionals in a relegation-bound Wolves team who included youngsters Mick Matthews, Bob Coy, John Pender and, for the only time, Irishman Tony Kernan. Picture courtesy of Coventry Evening Telegraph.

Hair-rising times for John Pender as he and Andy Gray challenge in the relegation scrap with Birmingham at Molineux on April 17, 1982. The young central defender had just broken into a Wolves team by now under the control of Ian Greaves following the departure of John Barnwell in the November. But he was thwarted here by Blues keeper Tony Coton's punch in a Midlands derby that finished 1-1, Gray scoring the home team's goal. Blues stayed up, Wolves didn't.

Down - and Up

John Pender shields the ball strongly during Wolves' emergence as a real mean machine in the early weeks of their life back in the Second Division. This 0-0 midweek draw at Chelsea in their first away game on August 31, 1982, was the first of eight successive League matches in which they kept a clean sheet. It was a determined response by Graham Hawkins's side after the club had nearly gone into extinction that summer. The Chelsea player in close up is Colin Lee, who was to return to Molineux as Mark McGhee's no 2 in 1995.

Wolves were locked in a run of four consecutive low-scoring draws when a Billy Kellock goal gave them a share of the honours on their trip to Derby on March 12, 1983. Alan Dodd, the gold-shirted player to the right, was one of the heroes of an unlikely promotion campaign while extrovert keeper John Burridge was another. He saves bravely here, protected by Geoff Palmer and John Humphrey. Picture courtesy of Derby Evening Telegraph.

John Burridge lives up to his crowd-pleasing image after a Wolves away win during their promotion run-in during the spring of 1983. The keeper was an ever-present and kept 20 clean sheets in the League, although the side - assembled on a low budget following the Bhatti brothers' 1982 takeover of the club - limped over the finishing in second place behind QPR, where they lost 2-1 in their final away match after clinching a top-flight place at Charlton five days before.

Wolves' stay back among the elite was brief and humiliating in 1983-84. This 3-1 win at Albion, which was shown on Match of the Day, was their first League victory of the season and came at the 15th attempt. It was a golden day for Danny Crainie, who has a gallery of Ken McNaught, Andy Blair, Martin Jol, Clive Whitehead, Wayne Clarke and Noel Luke as he scores the first of his two Hawthorns goals that were supplemented by one from Clarke.

Scot Danny Crainie leaps over the leg of Welshman Robbie James at Stoke on May 12, 1984, in what still stands as Wolves' last game in English football's top flight. Boss Graham Hawkins had been sacked a few weeks earlier and the side had been condemned to finishing bottom long before. Their points tally was a miserable 29 but this 4-0 defeat, in which Paul Maguire scored all four, was still significant in as much as it kept Stoke up and demoted Birmingham instead.

Colin Brazier, who had played 91 games for Wolves from 1976 to 1982, was in Walsall colours by the time of this snow-hit Third Division Sunday morning clash at Saddlers' old Fellows Park home on February 9, 1986. Dean Edwards is the challenging striker on the day Micky Holmes (in the background with Mark Taylor) scored for Sammy Chapman's side. Wolves were on the way to a third straight relegation and more brushes with extinction.

Seeds of recovery were evident when Fourth Division Wolves won 2-1 at Third Division Notts County in this Littlewoods Cup first-round second-leg clash on August 25, 1987. Graham Turner's side had won the first leg 3-0. Ex-Molineux hero Andy Gray, chased by Ally Robertson, threatens Mark Kendall at a time when Wolves fans were banned from away games because of crowd trouble at Scarborough on the first day of 1987-88. Picture courtesy of Nottingham Evening Post.

Wembley Revisited - Twice

WOLVERHAMPTON Wanderers had known much bigger Wembley occasions than the 1988 Sherpa Van Trophy final they lit up so spectacularly. But none had been more significant to them.

When the team fashioned by Graham Turner made it through a two-legged area final against Notts County, it was as if the club had re-established themselves in the football world.

They had spent several seasons lurching from one crisis to another, surviving going bust only by the skin of their teeth. They had become an embarrassment.

In their darkest hour, the club who had dominated the English League and conquered Europe in the 1950s even suffered the humiliation of a 3-0 FA Cup defeat against Multipart League side Chorley. They could surely stoop no lower. Thankfully, they didn't.

Recovery came with the careful management of Turner, the recruitment of a refreshing, loyal band of hungry players and, above all, the goals of Steve Bull.

Wolves were beaten in the Division Four play-off final of 1986-87 but they marched from the basement section as runaway champions the following year and had twin excursions to the Twin Towers.

They overcame Swansea, Bristol City, Brentford, Peterborough and Torquay as well as Notts County in the various rounds of the Sherpa Van and, through their excellent League form of the same winter, qualified to play at the sport's spiritual home in the Mercantile Credit Classic - a tournament staged over a mid-April weekend to celebrate the centenary of the Football League.

Wolves even had the satisfaction of drawing 1-1 with the then mighty Everton in the radical two-day event but that achievement and subsequent defeat on penalties was small beer compared with the Sherpa showdown with Burnley. That was big!

No fewer than 80,841 crammed into Wembley, including up to 50,000 bedecked in gold and black, to see Wolves win 2-0. And they didn't even need Bull to add to his stunning 52 goals for the season as goals by Andy Mutch and Robbie Dennison did the trick.

Wolves were back!

Wembley, with small pockets of fans from many different clubs, had an unreal air when it staged the Mercantile Credit centenary tournament in the spring of 1988, a few weeks before Wolves returned for the Sherpa Van Trophy final. Games were played over 20 minutes each way in two days of lengthy competition and Graham Turner's team rose to the occasion well before going out on penalties to Everton at the first hurdle. They drew 1-1 in normal time thanks to a Robbie Dennison special, Wayne Clarke having popped up between Andy Thompson, Ally Robertson, Floyd Streete and Gary Bellamy in the picture above to open the scoring.

Another happy Wolves night against Notts County on April 19, 1988 as Micky Holmes, Phil Robinson, Steve Bull and Keith Downing toast the booking of a Wembley place. John Barnwell's Magpies were brought down 3-0 in this Sherpa Van Trophy area final second leg at Molineux, Bull scoring twice on his way to an astonishing 52 goals for the season and ex-County man Downing once. Wolves had drawn 1-1 at Meadow Lane in the first leg. Picture courtesy of Nottingham Evening Post.

One of Wembley's last 80,000-plus crowds were present to see the all-Division Four Sherpa Van Trophy final between Wolves and Burnley on Sunday, May 29, 1988. And the lush acres of football headquarters were very much to the liking of Robbie Dennison, who curled in a delightful second-half free-kick for the killer goal in his side's 2-0 victory. Dennison, a regular in the team who comfortaby won the title nearly a month earlier, is pursued here by Burnley's former Molineux midfielder Peter Daniel, watched by Keith Downing.

Gary Bellamy, one of the quiet men of the successful team put together by Graham Turner, sinks to his knees as the whistle blows on Wolves' victory in the Wembley sunshine. The tall defender had arrived from Chesterfield the previous summer - around the same time as the also-pictured Phil Robinson, who was to prove a lucky omen in also getting his subsequent clubs to the Twin Towers.

Time to party! Midfielders Keith Downing and Nigel Vaughan show the silverware off to an estimated 45,000 Wolves fans on the ritual lap of honour. For Downing, it was a particularly sweet time - he was a Wolves fan before launching his playing career. Vaughan won ten senior Welsh caps but two other members of the Wembley squad, Micky Holmes and Steve Stoutt, were freed a few days later.

All action in Wolves' goalmouth as Keith Downing and no 5 Ally Robertson bravely block a close-range shot by Keith Alexander in the FA Cup first-round tie at Grimsby in November, 1988. From left, Andy Mutch, Nicky Clarke and Mark Venus are the other gold-shirted players on hand while Richard O'Kelly waits for possible crumbs. Promotion-bound Wolves, who were in a run of eight successive Third Division wins at the time, lost 1-0 to a goal direct from a corner. Picture courtesy of Grimsby Evening Telegraph.

Gary Bellamy and Nicky Clarke climb to challenge Devon White during Wolves' 0-0 Boxing Day draw against Bristol Rovers at Twerton Park on 1988. Steve Bull, who was to equal John Richards' club record of 194 goals at this venue in 1991-92, is on the left, Floyd Streete on the right and Mark Venus is the no 3. A week later, Molineux was to attract its first 20,000-plus gate for five years for the visit of Chester. Picture courtesy of Bristol Evening Post.

This Wolves effort was disallowed, but later goals by Steve Bull (his 50th of the season) and Robbie Dennison secured the 2-2 draw Graham Turner's men needed against Sheffield United on May 9, 1989, to clinch the Third Division title. Despite the deserted North Bank, there was a bumper 24,321 crowd as the Blades got the point they needed to be able to celebrate promotion. Wolves men pictured are Keith Downing, Andy Thompson and Andy Mutch while no 5 Paul Stancliffe (left) joined them a couple of years later.

Steve White sees a shot blocked by Alistair Robertson in the 3-1 defeat at Swindon shortly after Wolves' arrival in the Second Division in 1989. Unusually for that time, the game was played on a Sunday and it became a sad day for Shane Westley (left) when he was sent off. Robertson, an inspiring captain in the successive title triumphs, played only another two games for the club and so narrowly missed out on the extremely rare feat of playing League football in four different decades - the 1960s, 1970s, 1980s and 1990s.

It's a sickener for battling Wolves as manager's son Nigel Clough hooks in the winner for Nottingham Forest eight minutes from the end of the FA Cup third-round clash at the City Ground in January, 1992. Tom Bennett and Mike Stowell are the duo powerless to intervene as the club's miserable sequence in the competition continued. Forest were riding high at the time as a top-flight force and were beaten finalists against Tottenham the previous year. Picture courtesy of Nottingham Evening Post.

Wolves fans Lloyd Walton (left) and Steve Yates, both from Wednesfield and both members of Linthouse Wolves, go on to the pitch at Upton Park to make a touching tribute to former West Ham and England legend Bobby Moore before the Second Division game in March, 1993. It was the first match at the ground since the death of Moore, the nation's World Cup winning captain, from cancer - a passing mourned by football lovers everywhere.

End of the FA Cup road for Wolves and almost the end of the Molineux road for Graham Turner. Mark Rankine (left) and David Kelly do battle with Erland Johnsen as the club's exciting 1993-94 journey terminates with a 1-0 sixth-round Sunday exit at Chelsea after earlier victories over Crystal Palace, Port Vale and Ipswich. In a season of what was then big spending by First Division standards, manager Turner resigned after a 3-0 League defeat at Portsmouth two nights later.

Graham Taylor, having left the England job a few weeks earlier, is unveiled as Wolves' new boss by Jonathan Hayward in March, 1994. Long-serving secretary Keith Pearson and fellow director Billy Wright are also pictured.

Graham Taylor's only full Molineux season was just under way when Wolves went to Notts County on an August Sunday in 1994 and drew 1-1 thanks to this Andy Thompson penalty. In front of the expectant away fans, Steve Cherry almost keeps the ball out but no 10 David Kelly and no 4 Darren Ferguson were soon joining in the celebrations. Taylor led the club to the play-offs, where they lost to Bolton in the semi-final. Picture courtesy of Nottingham Evening Post.

David Kelly lunges forward through a cluster of markers and team-mates to head Wolves' killer second goal in the West Midlands derby against Albion at Molineux on August 28, 1994. This 69th minute effort from the Albion-supporting striker sealed a 2-0 win which left Wolves two places off the top of the table and their victims two places off the bottom. Also pictured are (from left) Paul Blades, Stuart Naylor, Mike Phelan, Neil Parsley, Peter Shirtliff, Daryl Burgess, Geoff Thomas and Neil Emblen. Former Albion man Andy Thompson had scored Wolves' opening goal from the penalty spot.

Some Fond Farewells

Ayresome Park, Middlesbrough is the setting as David Kelly slides in for a loose ball during Wolves' costly trip to the north-east in November, 1994. Graham Taylor's side had led the table for more than two months and were briefly to do so again a few days later. But this 1-0 defeat swung the issue the way of Bryan Robson's team, who took the only automatic promotion spot available that season.

Many English football grounds took on a new look in the 1990s with major redevelopment. Others went under the bulldozer as clubs opted to move to new out-of-town locations. As a result, Wolves found themselves visiting many old venues for the last time during that particular decade. This short section is dedicated to those final calls.......

Iwan Roberts, a thorn in Wolves' side before he joined them in the summer of 1996 and again after his departure a year later, gives Dean Richards a hard time during this aerial battle at Leicester in September, 1995. Sadly, the striker was not such a big success at Molineux and Mark McGhee was happy to recoup most of his money. Richards had upgraded his loan move from Bradford into a permanent deal during the summer of 1995 - a close season in which he figured alongside the likes of David Beckham and Phil Neville in the England side at the Toulon under-21 tournament. Wolves lost 1-0 on this, their last trip to Filbert Street and Graham Taylor's reign as manager was to last only a further two months.

SOME FOND FAREWELLS

Derby's Baseball Ground has been the setting for many a muddy battle for Wolves over the years and John de Wolf wasn't afraid to indulge in some dubious grappling when a side now under the control of Mark McGhee headed there in February, 1996. The Rams at the time were on their way to promotion but Wolves dug in for an honourable goalless draw.

It became known as the Battle of Burnden Park - and this is why. Around 20 players were involved in a heated fracas in the opening minutes of Wolves' First Division game at Bolton in January, 1997, and both clubs remained under the close spotlight of the FA's disciplinary watchdogs for a long time afterwards. Surprisingly, no-one was sent off or even booked as a consequence but the white-shirted Wanderers appeared to cope better than the gold and black version with the subsequent high feelings. They won 3-0, with Nathan Blake scoring one of their goals, and were to win the title by a huge 18 points. Wolves finished third and lost in the play-off semi-final.

The Keano Era

A teenager by the name of Robbie Keane exploded on to the Molineux scene in the summer of 1997 and was to enjoy two and a bit years of Wolves fame before moving on to make his fortune with Coventry, Inter Milan and Leeds, and become a big Republic of Ireland star. He scored 29 goals in 87 appearances for Wolves - the club he joined for nothing and left for six million. The first of the goals came from this left-foot fizzer (above) in a win at Norwich on the first day of 1997-98 and the last at home to Portsmouth in August, 1999 (below) in his final League outing for the club. Steve Sedgley is the player deciding that it's pointless chasing the precocious youngster!

The greatest moment in Wolves' recent history is secured by Don Goodman's 83rd minute shot, which beats England keeper Nigel Martyn for the only goal of the FA Cup sixth-round tie at Leeds on March 7, 1998. The victory, which followed earlier wins against Darlington, Charlton and Wimbledon, was even more special for Goodman as he used to be a ball-boy at Leeds, the club of his birthplace.

In front of a 39,372 Sunday lunchtime crowd at Villa Park, the big FA Cup dream was ended for Mark McGhee's Wolves by this 12th minute gift for Christopher Wreh. It was the only goal of a semi-final for which Robbie Keane and Steve Bull were both controversially left out of the starting line-up. But there was some consolation for Wolves in defeat. Victors Arsenal went on to beat Newcastle in the final, having already served up the League championship for manager Arsene Wenger. Also pictured are Steve Sedgley and Keith Curle.

Wolves' game at Bristol City on November 7, 1998, wasn't just notable for being Colin Lee's first as temporary manager following the departure of Mark McGhee. The astonishing 6-1 victory also made David Connolly only the third player from the club after Dennis Westcott and Steve Bull to score four times in an away League game. It was Wolves' biggest win on their League travels for 21 years and their highest tally in a game for six and a half years. As if that lot of statistics weren't enough, even further headlines were written after the club's mascot indulged in some extraordinary and not-so-friendly fisticuffs on the pitch during the half-time interval.

'Wolfie' found 'City Cat' a friendlier proposition than the three portly pigs and had cooled off by the time the second half of the game was about to start. Even so, there was talk of police action for some time and the astonishing story gathered momentum when pictures of the fighting were used in newspapers as far afield as Australia. Wolves were not slow to capitalise on the publicity and, for the home game against Sheffield United in the following midweek, the cuddly companion ran out to the tune from Rocky, posturing threateningly as he did so!

Looking to the Future

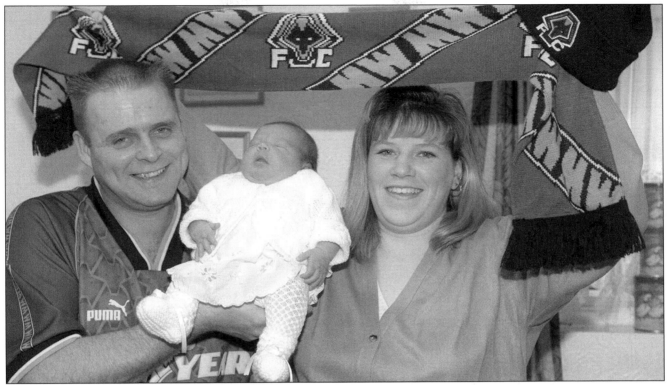

Keen Wolves supporters Steven and Tania Oliver had no hesitation when the new addition to their family arrived in the early winter of 1997-98. So strong was their dedication to the gold and black cause that there was only one name for their baby daughter......Molineux. The happy family were pictured at their home in the Stirchley district of Telford, where two of the threesome managed to stay awake during the photographer's visit!

Shropshire is again the setting in April, 1999, as Wolves' Australian duo Steve Corica (left) and Kevin Muscat, who both lived in the county during their time at the club, dropped in on Telford town centre for a signing session that went down well with local youngsters.

It may be the end of the season - but it's not really that warm! May, 1999, nevertheless proved to be torso-baring time for this Wolves supporter, who decided to put on a brave face during the club's narrow failure to reach the promotion play-offs under the new management of Colin Lee and John Ward. The duo had been on an extended trial since mid-winter but were told by Sir Jack Hayward straight after this final game at home to Bradford that they were to be handed permanent deals. The side under their command made a second spirited tilt the following year and again just missed out on a top-six finish despite winning 1-0 at Port Vale on the final day of the season.

Pre-season tours are the time for Wolves fans from various corners of England, mainland Europe and Scandinavia to join forces - and this jaunt to sunny Portugal was no exception. Supporters from different towns and countries are pictured in good voice during the 2-2 draw at Caldas, near Lisbon, in July, 2001. Great Western isn't so far away from Molineux - it's a pub in Wolverhampton!

Other titles available from Thomas Publications,
all written by David Instone, are:

The Bully Years (£8.99)

Wolves: Exclusive!(£6.99)

Sir Jack (£12.99)

For details of how to purchase, please write to:

Thomas Publications, PO Box 17, Newport,
Shropshire, TF10 7WT

This author has also written Wolverhampton Wanderers Greats
and helped compile Memories of Molineux,
The Only Way is Up, Harry's Game and
Who the Hell was Dudley Kernick?

Subscribers

Peter Abbott

Nick Jack George Abbotts

Bob Adams

Dave Adams

Jackie Adams

Lee Adams

Stephen Alcock

Marc Aldridge

Chris Aldritt

Luke Oliver Alexander

Geoff Allman

Douglas Allsop

M Alvarez-Garmon

Gerald Amos

Stuart Anson

Jason Asbury

Michael Ashmore

R P and P N Ashton

John Ashwood

Mark Astbury

R Astbury

Daniel Aston

Glenn A Aston

Derek Aylward

Sam Bagnall

Keith Baigent

Nigel Bailey

Terry Bailey

Trevor Bailey

Jim Bain

Adrian Baker

Alf Baker

Evelyn and John Baker

Paul Baker

Ross Baker

Shelly Baker

Matthew Bakewell

James Ball

Charles Bamforth

Rob Bancroft

Steven Banfield

David John Bannister

Mr C J Barber

Paul Barklam

Jeremy Bassett

Leslie Bate

John Bates

Thomas Baugh

Chris Bayley

Simon Bayley

Les Bayliss

Steve Bazeley

Leslie Beale

Kev Beardsmore

R J Bedward

Paul Bennett

Stephen Berridge

Simon Betteridge

Anthony Bevington

Anthony Bibb

Victor Bicknell

Andrew Bill

Edward Bill

Vic Billingham

SUBSCRIBERS

John Derek Birch

Peter Bishop

Soren C Bjulf

George Blackhall

Laurence Blackhall

Robert Blackhall

Mark Blagbrough

James Boddy

Norman Boden

Wayne Bood

Chris Booth

Patrick Bowen

Mick Bradbury

Karl Bradley

Stuart Bramall

Daniel Bremner

Tom Brindley

Adam Brinsdon

Ryan Bristow

Gordon Brookes

Michael Brookhouse

Ian Brooks

Carl Broome

David Broome

Basil Brown

Daniel Brown

Stuart Brown

W T Brown

Ray Buckler

Thomas Buckley

Ernie Bugelli

Paul Burden

David Paul Burrows

Ryan Martin Burt

Thomas Byrne

Stephen Cadman

Mark and Jo Cadwallader

Callum

Albert Camilleri

Mick Canning

Cannock Wolves

Don Carman

Martin Carroll

Peter Carter

Charles Cartwright

Fran Cartwright

Rebecca Cartwright

Simon Cartwright

Tim Cartwright

R Castle

Mike Chastney

Martin Chater

Jaz Chima

Nathan Chrimes

Murray Chrystal

Jan and Ali Clark

John Clarke

Andrew Cleaver

David Cleveland

R J Cleverly

Terence F Coles

David Collett

Ian Collett

Chris Collier

Andy Collins

Phil Colyer

G Cook

Geoff Cooper

FOREVER WOLVES

John Corfield

W H Corfield

Andrew Cox

Steven Cox

Bob Crockett

Reg Crook

John A Cross

Andrew Crowe

Rosemary Crump

Kenneth Dale

Stian Dalland

John Dallaway

Brian Daniels

John E Dannatt

James R Darke

Harry Davenhill

Alan Davies

Alan James Davies

Andrew J Davies

Caren Davies

Margaret Davies

Mark Kenneth Davies

Paul Davies

Roy S Davies

Keith Davison

Ian S Day

Peter Deans

Harold Degg

Alistair Dey

Philip Dodd

Ashley Dolan

B T Dorrell

Richard Dove

Tommy Dowds

Kevin Drew

Chris Driver

William Duddell

Luke Duggan

The Dungars

Andrew Dunn

Keith Dunn

Paul Wayne Dunne

Ian Eccles

Terry Edgeler

Aaron Edmonds

Martyn B Edwards

Sidney Edwards

Steve Elliott

David Mark Emery

Emma (Bermuda Wolves)

Dr Margaret W Emsley

Steve English

Alfred Evans

Christopher M Evans

Leslie Evans

Mel and Jenny Evans

Ryan Evans

Walter Evans

William Evans

Mark Everiss

Richard Farrow

Dean Fellows

Pat Fellows

Bill Fern

R R J Filkins

Judith Fish

Don Fisher

Jim Fisher (Yorkshire Wolves)

SUBSCRIBERS

Willie Fitzgerald

Andrew Flack

Richard J Flavell

Geir Foss

Paul Fowles

Rik Frampton

Daniel Gaichas

Colin Gannon

Maurice Gelipter

Richard Gill

F D Gilson (South London Harriers)

Pop Godfrey

David Goodhead

Steve Gordos

Joseph Grant-Bicknell

J B Green

Len Green

Paul Green

Robert H Green

Tony Green

Rob and Martin Gregory

David Grice

Alan Gripton

Ola Grue

Bjorn Gudbjornsson

Malcolm Guest

Stuart A Guest

Alan Haddock

Leon Haldren

Alan Hall

Joseph Peter Hands

Peter John Hands

Hannah and Richard

Sean Hare

P W Harman

Carl Harper

David Harper

Bernard Harris

Matthew Harris

Raymond Harris

Steve Harris

Alan Harrison

Daniel Harrison

Dave Harrison

Andy Hart

Steven Hartill

Darren Hartle

Wayne Hartshorne

John Harvey

Dave Haytree

Marcus Hayward

Michael Hayward

Wayne Hawthorne

Ron Head

Karmal Heer

Odin B Henrikssen

Kevin Hession

David Hewitt

William John Hickman

Gary Hill

Rod Hill

Stephen Neil Hill

Neil Hinton

Brian Hirst

Christopher Hirst

Ron Hodson

Brian Holden

Robert Holding

FOREVER WOLVES

Peter Holloway
Harry Holmes
Damian Homer
John Homer
Douglas Robert Hooper
Martin Horne
Paul Horton
Tim Hough
Andrew J Howe
David Huband
John Huband
David Hughes
Frank Hull
Ellie Jaye Humpage
K A Hunt
John D Hurd
Allen Hutt
Ralph Hyde
Clive James
Graham Jarman -
(in memory of Bill Jarman)
Stu Jarman
John Jarvis
Ronald Jasper
K M Jeffrey
Leighton Jenkins
Adam Jewkes
Mervyn J Jewkes
Neil Johnson -
(in memory of Oscar Johnson)
Wayne Johnson
Andrew Jones
Audrey Jones
Barry Jones

Darren Jones
Derek Edward Jones
Edward T Jones
F W Jones
Graham Jones
Kevin Jones
Malcolm Jones
Michael G Jones
Neil Harry Jones
Peter Jones
Philip Jones
Stuart P G Jones
Les Jordan
John Kedward
David Keeling
Dave Kersey
Robert Kiernan
Jim Kinniburgh
Anne P Knight
Vi Knight
Steve Knowles
R Kozakiewicz
John Lalley
John Lansley
Tom and Joe Lansley
Paul Robert Lancett
Michael W Lane
Peter Lansley
Ian Laschke
Terry Latewood
Shawn R Law
Ray Lees
Reg Lees
Michael Leng

SUBSCRIBERS

Brian Lewis

Evan Kirkley Lewis

Tony Lewis

Andrew Light

Knut Lindaas

John David Lloyd

Stephen Lounds

Owen James Lovett

Chris Lowe

Peter C Lowe

Simon Lucas

Stuart, Adam and James Lustigman

Curt Lycett

Joe Mackett

Sheran Macklin

Philip Magness

Ken Male

Craig Malone

Truls Mansson

L M Martin

Mark Martin

Ian Nicholas Mason

Nigel and Tim Mason

John Maule

Don McAliece

James McCrea

Iain McGuinness

Rob McLeod

Paddy McShane

Rob Meli

Sim Mellor

John Metcalfe

E 'Barrs' Millington

Brian Millward

Richard Milner

Amber Mincher

Peter Mitchell

Samantha Mock

Trond Møller

Molloy Family (Belfast)

Joan Moor

Lee Morgan

Peter Morgan

Alan Morris

D V Morris

Graham Ernest Morris

Keith Morris

Margaret Morris

Kenneth Munk

Andy Murden

Liam Murphy

Neil Murray

G Narraway

Dave Nash

Tim Nash

Barry Nicholls

Debbie Nicholls

Doreen Nicholls

Bob Nicholson

Lauren Nolan

Barry Norwood

John Nuttall

Per Erik Nygård

Jeff Oakley

Simon Oakley

Steven Oakley

Philip A J O'Connor

Darren Onions

FOREVER WOLVES

Laura Orves

Andy Overton

Keith Owen

Robert Owen

Stephen Owen

Colin Paddock

Eric Page

Phil Painter

Alison Palmer

Bernard and Joy Palmer

Anthony Parker

Kieran Parkes

John Parry

Stuart Parry

Simon Patten

Paul

Ronald Peacock

Roy Pearce

Douglas J Pearl

Leslie Graham Pearson

Nicholas Perks

Steve Perry

Bjorn Persson

Dave Phillips

Philip Pike

Dennis Plant

Richard Plant

Robert Plater

Matthew Plested

Kevin Ponder

Alan Poole

Charles Poultney

Robert Poulton

Michael John Powell

Kieren Pratty

Robert J Preece

Steven Richard Preece

Edward Price

Michael James Price

Peter C Price

Russell Price

Andrew Priest

Chris Pritchard

M A Pritchard

Martyn Pritchard

Dorothy Prosser

Bryan Dean Pulcella

Tommy Purslow

Dale Race

Clifford Raison

Neil Raphael

Dave Rawlings

Andrew Raybould

Mike Redfern

Ian Redmond

Gordon Terence Reed

Brian Restall

Gavin Reynolds

Paul Richards

Ian Ritchie Jnr

Veli Rnkovic

Martin Roberts

Mark G Robinson

Paul 'Aka' Robinson

Alan Roe

David Rook

Matt Rothwell

Norman W Round

SUBSCRIBERS

Laura Rowley

Arthur and Jane Rudge

Patrick Rynn

Mike Salmon

A E Salusbury

Philip Samosa

Michael Sampson

David Sanders

Kerry Sargeant

Peter Saunders

Mark Sawbridge

Brian W Scott

Ian Sharp

Tony Shelton

Ken Sherwood

Dennis Shingler

Terry Shinton

Maurice Shipley

Ian Shutt

M Sidbotham

Andy Simmons

Barry Simms

Dave Slape

Lee Slater

Nicholas Small

William Small

David J Smart

Keith Smith

Patrick J Smith

Reg Smith

W A Smith

Svein Solberg

Ian Sommerville

Roy Spencer

Roger Stanton

H J and C J Staples

Adrian P Starkey

Robert Steadman

Håvard Steen

Ian Stevens

John G Steventon

Margaret and Jean Stokes

Dagfinn Stokkenes

Andy Strange

David Summers

Owen and Hayley Tanner

The Tate Family

John Taylor

Jonathan L Taylor

Laura Taylor

Robert E Taylor

Øyvind Teige

Gary Thomas

John Thomas

Martin J Thomas

Michael Thomas

R J Thomas

Martin Thompson

Brian Timmis

John Timmis

Matthew Tomkinson

Rachel Tomkinson

David Allen Tomlinson

Les Tonkinson

Graham Tonks

Neil Totty

Andrew Troath

Adrian Turner

FOREVER WOLVES

Barry W Turner

Edward Turner

Glenn K Turner

J J Turner

Mark Turner

Matthew James Andrew Turner

Melvin Turner

Melvin (Angus) Turner

Phil Turner

Tony Turpin

George Voulgaris

Michael Wainwright

Edward Wakeley

Kevin Waldron

Albert Walker

Bayley Martin Walker

Michael Walsh

Tyrone Walsh

G T Walters

Simon Walters

Steve Warner

Dave Wassell

Alfred Watkins

George Webster

Andrew Wedge

Andrew George Wells

Peter Wells

Steven Wells

John Wenzel

David M Westley

Dennis Weston

Ian S Weston

Stephen P Weston

Craig Westwood

Damion Westwood

Ken Westwood

Mike Westwood

Nathan Westwood

Sarah Westwood

Peter J Wheeler

Adrian Whitehurst

Howard Whittingham

Helen Wicking

Dr S J H Wilkes

Neil Wilkes

Thomas Wilkinson

Michael Willets

Judith A Williams

Paul Williams

Peter Williams

Rachel M Williams

Philip Willis

David Winchurch

W E Wisedale

John Withers

Don Wolvey

Kevin J Woodall

W D Worrall

Keith Worton

Alex R Wright

Andrew L Wright

Michael Wright

Steve (Yorkshire Wolves) Wright

Tony Wright

Mark Alan Wylde

Lyndon York

Paul P Young

Cyril Young